Without Regret

Be more, see more, achieve more that really matters

J. Michael Godfrey, DMin, PhD, PCC

THOMAS NOBLE BOOKS

427 N Tatnall Street #90946
Wilmington, DE 19801-2230

Library of Congress Control Number: 2013940194

ISBN 978-0-9892357-1-6

Printed in the United States of America

This publication is designed to provide accurate and authoritative information in regard to the subject matter covered. It is sold with the understanding that the author is not engaged in rendering professional services. If legal, accounting, medical, psychological, or any other expert assistance is required, the services of a competent professional person should be sought. Client names have been changed to protect identities.

Advance Praise for *Without Regret*

"It's never too late to do away with regret and be uniquely you. In *Without Regret*, J. Michael Godfrey offers his readers the tools they need to live a life without regrets and become the persons they were uniquely created to be. Integrating his years of training, education, coaching, and local church ministry, Godfrey provides helpful and practical steps to be more, see more, and achieve more that really matters. He reminds us that regret focuses our attention on the past, but with hard work and great courage we can live purposefully in the present and transform our future. With keen insight Godfrey guides his reader to form a life plan based upon who they are and to live out that plan with courage, integrity, and grace. *Without Regret* is a timely message for those who struggle with the demands of faith, family, and work. You won't regret the journey that awaits."

Rev. Dr. Wade E. Smith, Ph.D., Pastor, First Baptist Church, Norman, Oklahoma

"As a football coach, I drilled the concepts of integrity, purpose, and achievement into my teams. *Without Regret* distills these concepts and many more into a practical and intelligent read. *Without Regret* tackles many issues common to our times: productivity, communication, burn-out, sabotage, and how to live a life you design instead of a life that just happens to you. Full of action plans and how-to steps that anyone can implement, *Without Regret* will make you a better person and a winner at the game of life. Highly recommended."

Grant Teaff, Executive Director, American Football Coaches Association

"Being yourself requires courage. *Without Regret* provides unique insights related to how we can answer the question "Who am I?" Once discovered, Mike candidly illustrates how each of us can live our lives with integrity, even while glimpsing at the rear-view mirror."

Brian L Fowler, MD, author of *The Beating of My Hearts*

"Michael Godfrey has given us a straightforward guide for improving our lives. Whatever your life stage, it is never too late to break the "regret" cycle. This accessible and practical guide gives you the tools you need to start this process. Useful for youth groups, college classes, church small groups, and individuals, Godfrey sets us on a path toward freedom."

"Living a life without regret is a universal desire. This book gives us a clear blueprint for making that desire a reality."

"From the opening sentence, I identified with the message in *Without Regret*. Dr. Godfrey's experience and study have prepared me to analyze my priorities, belief systems, and attitude in order to live a more fulfilling life. Just as he writes of the need to consistently plan and re-evaluate, I plan to use *Without Regret* as a tool for doing so for many years to come."

"For years I've been trying to put a handle on why I feel the way I do when looking back over my shoulder. I mean, what parent hasn't felt some aspect of regret in raising kids? Did I say the right thing? Was I fair? Did I live up to my words? And thinking back on my high school and college years, I've wondered if a different choice might have made for a different outcome. Truth is, I'm here now. It's time to leave regrets where they belong... behind me. Mike's given me some real tools here to deal with 'the now' of life; to embrace the uniqueness that God has planted in me. I'm sure everyone who reads this book will come away, as I did, with real, practical and positive help for steps to a life without regret."

"In a world filled with measurements and pressures of success from the outside world ranging from personal relationships, career, power and monetary goals, the book *Without Regret* gives a step-by-step plan to evaluate and match your belief system to a life plan that brings a constant inner joy that is sustainable instead of fleeting happiness and recurrent guilt. A great read."

Kimber L. Holmes, DDS, Pasadena Family Dentistry, Pasadena, Texas

"*Without Regret* speaks to the core of what holds us back from regret-free living. Dr. Godfrey's unique perspective of having coached hundreds of people from all walks of life, coupled with his transparency in sharing his own life experiences, makes *Without Regret* a must-read."

Chuck King, Owner, Chick-fil-A, Longview, Texas

"Michael Godfrey has provided for us a practical and valid path toward the abundant life promised to people of faith. He lays out a wonderfully detailed variety of ways for people to frame the process of self-discovery and how it is fundamental to the journey of living a life without regret. This is more than just another self-help book. It's an easily accessed, but highly thoughtful template for faithful living."

Charles Fuller, DMA, MDiv, Interim Administrative Pastor and Minister for
Congregational Life, Second Baptist Church, Little Rock, Arkansas

"Life moves at such a fast pace – *Without Regret* will help many people focus on present and future, not past. Without such a focus, much of life may be wasted on regrets of 'what if.' Michael has done a great job with this book of helping the reader look forward, reducing the drag of the past, and giving all to the capacity God has provided us with in each day of life. The tools to accomplish free living are contained in this book; go forward in Christ!"

Tom Crow, Executive Pastor, First Baptist Church, Nashville, Tennessee

"*Without Regret* has been a powerful reminder to me that I have a choice when it comes to regret and that no one can make me feel regret. In addition, Michael's disciplines of Forming, Performing, and Transforming provided me with a practical approach to transform regret into a potential-filled experience. I am eager to carve out time to apply these disciplines."

J. Val Hastings, Founder and President, Coaching4Clergy, author of *Ministry 3.0*

"*Without Regret* speaks to real life. Dr. Godfrey's wise words have produced laser-like focus for living and are enabling me as a Christ-follower, wife, mother and minister to literally live without regret."

Julie Hammer, Minister of Childhood Education,
Columbus Avenue Baptist Church, Waco, Texas

"Churches are filled with Christians who are living life with regret. This book is a useful tool for pastors seeking practical steps to help their parishioners learn to embrace their God-given uniqueness and to live life without regret."

Rev. Jeff Cockerham, Associate Pastor of Discipleship,
Central Baptist Church, Fountain City, Tennessee

"Each of us experiences some measure of regret and disappointment in our lives. In *Without Regret*, Michael inspires us to form, perform and transform our lives in order to achieve a life of abundance and experience all of the blessings that God has in store for us."

Ian McCaw, Director of Athletics, Baylor University

"*Without Regret* gave me insight into my past, present, and future pursuits. It helped me evaluate what I need to do and how to make necessary changes to achieve what really matters to me. It makes me realize that 'I'm not where I should be, but I'm a long way from where I used to be,' but with lots of room for continued improvement. *Without Regret* will help me keep my focus."

Colonel Don Riley, USAF Retired, Waco, Texas

"Having experienced regret and yet not living with regret is such a difficult difference to discover that most of us can never distinguish the two. The difference is not found in philosophical soliloquy but in practical steps as Dr. Godfrey lays out so clearly, concisely, and convincingly. After reading Michael's *Without Regret* I can confidently say that I know the difference of experiencing regret yet not living with regret, and I am now living 'without regret.'

Glynn N. Stone, PhD, Senior Pastor, Mobberly Baptist Church, Longview, Texas

"Having known Michael Godfrey both personally and professionally, I can attest first hand to the fact that the principles and wisdom set forth in *Without Regret* work. Michael is well-qualified and dead-on in his insight. Application of the Form - Perform - Transform model will make an immediate impact on your life, just like it has in mine!"

Mark Whitaker, JD, Partner, Baird, Crews, Schiller & Whitaker, P.C., Temple, Texas

"I consider Michael a dear friend and mentor. His wisdom and perspective have helped change my leadership skills and allowed me to grow both professionally and spiritually. I was moved while reading *Without Regret* by the concept that 'regret is your choice.' Grasping the truth of that statement opened up my mind to the principle that I have a lot more power over regret than regret has power over me!"

Rev. Amos Humphries, Senior Pastor,
Park Lake Drive Baptist Church, Waco, Texas

"I have worked with Michael on a church staff, and enjoyed many conversations with him about life and work. *Without Regret* captures the wisdom of his personal spiritual journey. Michael has clearly discovered many gems along the ups and downs of his path, and he does an excellent job of offering these to the reader. This book will be of great help to those who find themselves second-guessing life while it continues to go by."

Rev. Wesley M. Eades, Ph.D. LPC, LMFT

"In my work as a licensed professional counselor, I have met with many individuals who are living in the pain of their own poor choices. Some people can struggle against this pain for years, due to a lack of understanding about how to move forward. In his book, *Without Regret*, Michael Godfrey lays out a framework for people to use as a way of addressing their regrets and making the necessary adjustments to live life more fully and more authentically. Each chapter also offers the opportunity to integrate matters of faith and spirituality into the transformation process. I found Dr. Godfrey's book to be both insightful and practical for those seeking resolution in moving past the pain of past regrets."

Tracy Miller, M.S., LPC, Pathway Counseling Center

"Michael, thank you for placing a mirror in my hand and guiding me through identifying and understanding the reality of regret in my life; and then providing practical, purposeful ways to move beyond it!"

Gaye Christy, Executive Assistant to the President, East Texas Baptist University

"In our present age, we all too often feel adrift, helpless to resist the waves of life and where those currents may take us. Dr. Godfrey's *Without Regret* sounds the horn that by changing our perspective we may chart a course and voyage to a destination of God's choosing."

Rev. Jim Coston, Senior Pastor, Calvary Baptist Church, Waco, Texas

"In the same way Jesus asked the paralytic, 'Do you wish to be healed?' *Without Regret* challenges us to choose to live a life without disappointment or regret. The answer is in the question. The message of the book is both simple and brilliant."

Todd Moore, CEO and Chairman of the Board,
Alliance Bank of Central Texas, Waco, Texas

"In this easy to read book, Michael Godfrey takes a complex issue and disassembles it into smaller, more manageable pieces. Risking oversimplification for our sake, he does the important work of convincing us that we can, indeed, overcome regret one 'do-able' step at a time. He walks alongside the reader as an experienced and reliable guide from the very first page onward. Here, Dr. Godfrey extends a helping hand. Pick up the book and grasp it."

Terry W. York, DMA, Professor of Christian Ministry and Church Music,
George W. Truett Theological Seminary, Baylor University, Waco, Texas

"In *Without Regret*, Michael Godfrey has taken on a topic or, more precisely, an emotion familiar to almost everyone, but that few have the knowledge, skills or understanding with which to successfully cope. This book convinced me to reassess my own emotional and spiritual maturity and to take an introspective look at how I deal with regret. Importantly, *Without Regret* does not offer some new 'pop psychology' mantra or questionable self-help methods; rather, the book provides some clear, concise and time-tested tools for use in living a life without regret. Yes, it can be done!! Thank you, Dr. Godfrey, for providing a work that encouraged and inspired this reader to adjust my own beliefs about regret and, in so doing, to make a conscious decision to live a life full of joy as I press on toward the goal. God bless!"

Rogers Pope, Jr., JD, Vice Chairman and Chief Operating Officer,
Texas Bank and Trust, Longview, Texas

"Is it possible to live a life without regret? After reading Dr. Godfrey's book, I believe it is. Dr. Godfrey presents a strategy that anyone can use to make decisions that lead to fulfillment rather than regret. In addition, his strategy provides a way to navigate the unexpected events of life so that feelings of regret become opportunities for learning. I am excited to discover what happens in my life as I begin to live without regret."

Marcy Smith, Minister of Children and Education,
Western Heights Baptist Church, Waco, Texas

"Michael Godfrey has written a marvelously wise book that offers concrete steps for resolving the regrets that come in life that can hamper our effectiveness, cramp our relationships, or put us out of commission altogether. Everyone who has ever said 'I wish that I had not done that,' or 'I am heartbroken that this happened,' will benefit enormously from reading this guide for promoting a more constructive, spiritual attitude toward life."

David E. Garland, Ph.D., Dean, Charles J. and Eleanor McLerran Delancey Chair of the Dean, and Professor of Christian Scriptures, George W. Truett Theological Seminary, Baylor University, Waco, Texas

"Michael Godfrey is a man of wisdom gifted in sharing his wisdom with others. *Without Regret* distills his wisdom into book form to share with all who will listen as they read. As a product of Dr. Godfrey's coaching, I highly recommend *Without Regret*. Read this book, practice its principles, and see growth flourish in your life."

Rev. Mike Lee, Senior Pastor, Third Baptist Church, Murfreesboro, Tennessee

"Michael's work in this book will guide you to peel back the layers of your life to find the authentic you. By peeling back the layers of your 'onion' you might just find a bud at the center just ready to blossom into what God intended you to be."

Kay Kotan, ACC, You Unlimited, Independence, Missouri

"My friend Michael Godfrey has coached me through some life altering transitions in recent years. This book contains the principles which now help me to live a maximized life, without regret!"

Jason Greene, Pastor, Heritage Church, Preston, UK

"In *Without Regret* Dr. Michael Godfrey brings his considerable skill in professional coaching and his solid background in adult learning and psychology to bear upon the central human struggle with meaning. The book guides the reader in specific ways to examine questions of personal uniqueness and calling and to make clear plans that will transform the future. I found this book to be encouraging and practical – a source of real help."

"Occasionally a book comes along that instantly absorbs the reader because you know the author has stood in your shoes a good while. *Without Regret* is just such a book, enumerating three simple but practical steps to springing forward – rather than falling apart – from failures and unmet expectations."

"Anyone who has lived, probably has experienced regret. Although many are minor in the grand scheme of things, there are some life experiences that overwhelm us with regret. If your regret is more of the latter variety than the former, then this book is for you. Dr. Godfrey provides the reader with a clear, concise strategy for moving forward in those times of guilt and regret, as well as for avoiding any future pitfalls related to them."

"Suppose there was a map that showed a path toward the integration of experience, purpose and hope. Suppose a life without regret wasn't a matter of happenstance but of decision and action. Would you use the map? Would you make a plan and move forward? Michael Godfrey's book *Without Regret* offers practical direction and helpful encouragement to all who are ready to take responsibility and risk for the outcome of their life and legacy. Intriguing, inspiring – a good read that you won't regret!"

The Reverend Suzan Hawkinson, M.Div.,
D.Min The First Presbyterian Church of Deerfield, Illinois

"Whether we realize it or not, regret hijacks our ability to make the most of the opportunities in front of us. In *Without Regret*, Michael Godfrey provides simple, yet profound steps for regaining control over our attitudes, our plans, and ultimately, our lives. By following the steps in this book, I am making small adjustments to my daily routine that help bring my actions in line with my values, thus setting me free from regret and free for making the most of my days."

Taylor Sandlin, D.Min., Pastor, Southland Baptist Church, San Angelo, Texas

"*Without Regret* addresses the most basic and strategic adjustment in maturing lives – discovering how to live according to your unique purpose and developing a plan for effectiveness and meeting the basic challenges in life. It is one of the most helpful guides I have read for meeting challenges and disappointments that often sidetrack us. This book will be a very significant guide for all professionals who desire to be more effective in their personal lives and careers."

Ronald L. Cook, Ph.D., Associate Professor of Christian Scriptures
and Director of the D.Min. Program, George W. Truett Theological Seminary,
Baylor University, Waco, Texas

"*Without Regret* confronts the reality that many of us simply – and very often regretfully – accept what life might bring our way. Drawing upon his personal experiences as well as insight gained from his many years as a life coach and mentor, author J. Michael Godfrey challenges the reader to begin now to live with genuine purpose and intentionality. In *Without Regret* you will find stimulating, creative and practical guidance that if followed, will indeed give you the opportunity to live a life that really matters – a life lived without regret!"

"*Without Regret* is an eye-opening book that showed me insights about myself and others I may have never understood. The idea that a regret-free life is found by regularly evaluating and making adjustments to be true to myself is invigorating. I am now able to live life with more freedom and confidence in the 'real' me!"

"*Without Regret* provides a simple, memorable outline for assessing your current life stage and station so you may address past or present regrets and avoid future and final regret. The principles outlined in *Without Regret* by Michael have been tested and proven out of personal and professional experience and will provide valuable guidance for anyone who wants to finish life's journey without regret."

"I really thought I had very few regrets in my life... man was I surprised. I never realized how much the regrets were affecting my true calling until I read this book. Godfrey nailed it: 'Regret was drying up my soul.' I have personally put the exercises that are encouraged into practice. The bottom line: it's transforming and renewing my self-concept, vision, and purpose. This book is like a breath of fresh mountain air for the soul."

Table of Contents

Introduction

Is this all that there is?

Have you ever asked yourself this dangerous question, maybe deep in the night when you can't sleep?

You've worked hard and have some achievements under your belt, yet you feel a quiet sadness or disappointment over lost opportunities, superficial relationships, missed moments with friends and family, or things you've said or done.

That's regret.

Regret is feeling that you missed out on what you really wanted while you were busy doing what you thought you had to do to survive. When you have feelings of regret you probably also believe that others are happy, fulfilled, and don't have regret.

Whether your regret is a twinge when you think of how you always wanted to pursue a certain profession, or is overwhelming—the throbbing pain of a lost love or a damaged relationship with your child—you're not alone.

In my career of serving people, I've come to see regret as a huge "Uh-oh" sensation people experience when they realize they have allowed life to carry them along past their real dreams, hopes, and desires. Regret can be a dark secret that keeps people stuck and living quietly in pain, believing that they don't deserve anything different or that it's too late to make important changes to move past it.

Let me tell you about Emily. When I first met Emily, she was swimming in regret. She had a child when she was in high school. Even though she worked hard to complete her education and build a career, she regretted her late start and the decisions she made as a teen. Emily felt behind her peers, inferior, and that she was not living up to her potential. Her regrets were sapping her energy and passion, and made her try too hard in every area of her life.

And maybe you know someone like Joel. Joel is a highly successful businessman with a great family. But he fears becoming like his father, who ignored his family to climb to the pinnacle of his profession and ended his life regretting the missed soccer games, camping trips, and family vacations. Joel does not have many regrets now, but he wants to proactively ensure that his life turns out differently from his father's.

Whether you are like Emily, weighed down by regret today, or you want to avoid its bitter taste in the future as Joel does, this book will help you.

You may be thinking you don't have time to plan to avoid regret or resolve the regret you already have. This is the most common excuse I hear from people about personal development. But think about the logic behind the statement "I don't have time to live without regret." Is this true for you? If so, you are resigned to live with it. You really do have time, but you are choosing to do something else with the time you have. You have elevated something else to a priority above planning and prioritizing in order to live with integrity and focused purpose, and without regret.

Your life is speeding faster and faster toward your final day. There are only so many opportunities to be all you want to be and do all you want to do. Life is too short to be crippled by regret and miss the things that really matter to you while you are busy with your to-do list.

You can learn to be more, see more, and achieve more that really matters—in your personal life, relationships, and pursuits. In *Without Regret*, you'll discover how to skillfully craft a life without regret through careful planning, courageous action, and renewed perspective.

To live a life without regret you will want to do three things:

Step 1. FORM a plan based on a clear understanding of who you are and why you are here

Step 2. PERFORM your plan courageously

Step 3. TRANSFORM your regret into a learning opportunity for living a hopeful, meaningful, and purposeful life.

I'm confident these steps work because they've been proven in my life and in the lives of my clients. This book is a culmination of all my years of study and work—drawing from personal experience, academic research, theoretical roots, and the faith that is such a deep and integral part of my life.

While I share my own experiences in these pages, I know that others (perhaps you) have had greater challenges than I. No matter what your challenge, the principles for a life without regret are universal. They are simple, but not easy. This book and these principles are not for the faint-hearted, but for the courageous person who is ready to experience all the meaning and abundance life has to offer.

These principles will empower you to avoid as much regret as possible and walk with focus and determination through what might otherwise be regrettable situations. They will help you see what's holding you back and help you *be* more, *see* more, and *achieve* more of what really matters to you.

And that, my friend, is what living "without regret" is all about.

Chapter 1

What is Regret?

Man is disturbed not by things but by the view he takes of them.
—Epictetus, Greek Stoic Philosopher

Regret is a word you probably don't use very often; you might use these more common words or phrases to express regret:

Sorry

Disappointed

Heartbroken

I hate that...

I wish that...

Think about the last time you felt regret. How would you describe the experience? Words like *fun, pleasant, encouraging,* and *enjoyable* are not likely a part of your description. So what is regret anyway?

Regret is comprised of emotions that surface when thoughts or behaviors—your own or those of others—or life events don't line up with your belief system. These emotions can also arise when your belief system seems to fail you as a guide for living and relating.

What Do Emotions Have to Do with Regret?

Emotions come in broad categories: mad (frustration, anger), sad (disappointment with self or others; grief over loss, great or small), afraid (of threat; of future; of loss of control), surprise (which can also be positive or pleasant), disgusted, happy, and excited.

You've probably heard people say, "It makes me feel..." Or, "He/she makes me feel..." You might want to make someone else responsible for the way you feel, pleasant or unpleasant. But blaming is an irresponsible approach to life.

You are responsible for your own emotions. No one *makes* you feel angry, sad, afraid, or happy. And, most important, no one makes you feel regret. When the emotions of regret arise in you, you have a choice about what to do—you can obsess and bathe in the negative emotions of regret or you can acknowledge it, name it, and move forward toward more productive things.

Taking responsibility for your emotions is a first step in learning to live without regret. Recognizing the context of those emotions takes you even farther down the road.

The context is set by your belief system, which is made up of opinions, principles, religious concepts, precepts, values, expectations, and convictions regarding what you believe to be true about yourself, others, relationships, and how the world works. Your belief system helps you make sense of it all. It serves as a guide for your choices and actions. As you interpret the world around you, you make decisions based on your interpretation about how you will live and relate in the world.

Theoretically, **without a belief system there is no reason for regret,** since you would have no particular way of seeing things and no definitions for what is "acceptable" and "regrettable" to you.

How Did I Get My Belief System?

In early childhood we develop beliefs by interacting with others and our environment. When these interactions are safe, healthy, loving, and appropriate, we develop healthy beliefs such as a sense of trust, hope, autonomy, purpose, and competence.

During childhood and teen years we gain the capacity to develop our beliefs through logical, concrete processes of thought. The beliefs of family, authority figures, and friends make sufficient sense that we adopt them, somewhat indiscriminately, into our system. You can probably remember some of the beliefs you had as a teenager that are no longer part of your belief system. At that age we lack the cognitive ability and experience to think about them critically, so we don't question them.

During late teen years and early adulthood we gain the cognitive ability to think abstractly and critically. This blossoming ability allows us to look at how our belief system serves us in making sense of experiences and making them fit together in a coherent manner. In adulthood, personal reflection is an essential activity for developing and molding our belief systems.

In *Forms of Intellectual and Moral Development in the College Years: A Scheme* and "Cognitive and Ethical Growth: The Making of Meaning" from The Modern American College, we learn from W. G. Perry that as we reach early adulthood and what are commonly known as the years of higher education, we want authorities to give us the "right" answers, only to discover that there are many "right" answers and that we must evaluate the data for ourselves and commit to what we believe. And we must repeat this process over and over again throughout life.[1]

Unfortunately, many do not do this. They stop with the idea or belief that what someone told them was "right." Stopping here is a bad idea. It is important to continue to develop your beliefs throughout your life by critically examining the validity, truth, and helpfulness of each belief and how it integrates with your system. It's hard to make sense of self, relationships, and life as a whole when using borrowed beliefs. It's like wearing borrowed eyeglasses. Your vision is limited and blurry— they just don't work for you.

Your belief system sets you up to experience a variety of emotions about life events. Some of these emotions are positive and contribute to a sense of security. Others, like regret, are unpleasant and disorienting.

> *It is very obvious that we are not influenced by "facts"*
> *but by our interpretation of facts.*
>
> —Alfred Adler, Psychologist

When our own actions, the actions of others, or circumstances of life do not fit with our belief system, we can feel emotions of regret. The feeling is unpleasant and we want relief from it. We might also become confused or disoriented regarding our beliefs. Sometimes we need to adjust our belief framework in order to make our experiences fit together and make sense again, which eases the pain of regret. Such critical examination and adjustment is essential if we are to continue to function well. And as I'm sure you've seen, a situation that shakes one person's belief system may not have the same effect on someone with a different system.

When people experience tragic loss they sometimes ask, "Why would

God do this?" or "Why would God let this happen?" Their belief system is not working for them. They believe God is loving and controls everything, and since He controls everything, He is also responsible for everything, including this tragedy. How can He be a loving God and do this?

These individuals have a choice. They can adjust their belief system to include that God is not responsible for everything, thus not in control of everything. Or they can continue to believe that God is in control of everything, therefore is not loving or must have some loving reason for perpetrating this tragic, senseless thing. Or their beliefs can be some combination of these.

When your own words and actions clash with your examined belief system, you can feel guilty or disappointed with yourself. When you transgress an unexamined, inherited belief system, however, you might feel shame, since that system belongs to someone else and you are hearing that person's shaming voice (versus your own voice of reason).

It's very important to question your beliefs. Sometimes a shaken belief system produces a simple change of thinking that's needed or a return to an original way of thinking. When confronted with the inadequacies of your belief system, you might wish you had known or believed something different, and experience regret. Either way, shaking the system is a good thing.

Some of the inherited beliefs you currently hold can be more of a problem than a help. When examined critically, you might discover that these beliefs contain little truth and don't provide the help you need to make sense of life or helpful guidance that leads to good outcomes. In fact, some beliefs you hold could be lies that cripple your living.

For example, you might believe that you can only be happy when everything is going your way, but upon careful examination discover that this belief allows for very little happiness, and that happiness is a choice, regardless of circumstances.

Other inherited beliefs are likely valid, good, and helpful, but you haven't examined them and made them your own. You keep them because "somebody said so."

For example, perhaps you read somewhere that the cheapest car is the one you are driving now and that buying a new car every few years is more expensive, so you have done this for years because you believe it and it continues to prove true.

Then there is the tested belief. When my mouth ran wild as a teenager, my dad would say, "Sometimes the least you can say the better off you'll be." I have tested this and found it to be true. I use the principle because I believe it, not because my dad said so.

Through critical reflection you can discover that an inherited belief is an excellent principle by which to live. Hold inherited beliefs only because you have tested them, truly believe them, and they work for you, not just because "somebody said so."

When Beliefs Don't Work for Guidance

Your belief system serves to guide your living. Some aspects of your belief system may be more consistent with reality than others, and some may be more helpful than others. Everyone has a combination of better and worse beliefs in their system. If your belief system is leading you to do things you later regret, then it's time to reexamine your system.

The belief systems of many adults are infested with narrow, hardened expectations and unexamined assumptions that don't help them understand and integrate life events into their experience. These beliefs provide poor guidance for living and relating. As a result, feelings of regret can arise.

Here's an example. I used to think that if those around me really loved me, they would know my needs and meet them. I expected that they could intuit my needs if they really cared enough. This is a common but unhelpful belief in regard to experiencing quality relationships. It wasn't consistent with reality and did not serve me well at all. Then, through critical reflection, I came to a different belief: "I cannot expect anyone to intuit my needs. I must communicate my needs to them."

What If My Beliefs Don't Fit My Experience?

It often comes as a surprise when life events, behaviors, and opinions you encounter don't fit with your belief system. The surprise is especially big when you are so confident in your beliefs that you have never evaluated them. When you discover the inadequacies of your belief, you think, "How could I have believed that?" and feel regret.

For example, let's say you were taught that normal people are socially outgoing and enjoy being with lots of people most of the time. Though you prefer to spend time alone or with a few others, and are not very outgoing, you work hard to be "normal." This leaves you exhausted much of the time. You experience regret that "normal" doesn't work for you. You wonder if something must be "wrong" with you. You must choose to either continue to try to be "normal" or adjust your belief system. If you carefully examine your belief about what is normal, you will discover that this belief is not based in truth and you can adjust your belief to make your life more enjoyable. You can then spend time alone or with a few close friends without feeling inadequate or abnormal.

Or maybe you believe that the best thing you can do for your family is provide a high standard of living. You believe your work is of the highest importance, so you work hard and go home in the evening with no energy left for your family. After ten years, you've lost your grip on the relationship you now want with your family. You look back to discover that your belief about work was not helpful and was even damaging, and that presence with your family was more important than a high standard of living. You will likely experience regret.

Even in the face of such regret, some people don't adjust. Like trying to drive down the road in a car with a crooked wheel (or two, or three), they tightly hold to conventional beliefs taught them in their childhood and teen years that no longer serve a full and rich experience of life. Many get stuck here, living in a belief system from their pre-adult years, using someone else's beliefs and values without having examined them or put them to the test.

Healthy adults continually adjust their belief systems as they have new experiences in life. It is important to develop a lifelong habit of proactively and rigorously examining the belief system you call yours. As you examine your beliefs, you will discard some ideas, modify some, and reaffirm some, thus adjusting your lens to make better sense of your experiences as you view them, and establishing a helpful framework for living. Even if until now your belief system has led to regret, you can go forward without it.

Chapter 2

What Does It Mean to Live without Regret?

Get correct views of life, and learn to see the world in its true light.
It will enable you to live pleasantly, to do good, and,
when summoned away, to leave without regret.

—Robert E. Lee

Living with regret exacts a high price from every aspect of your being. Physically, you might be tense, sore, achy, unmotivated, and fatigued. Emotionally, you are more likely to experience anger and depression. Socially, you might be withdrawn or more "out there" in order to gain support. Spiritually, regret dries up the soul. When you live with regret, it shows up in the tone and energy of your voice. It can show up in your conversation as you air your grievances aloud with others, which to them may be unpleasant.

Just yesterday my wife and I were at a local store, and the checker's anxiety was high enough that while scanning our purchases he complained about store policy and management to us—strangers. Maybe you don't share your regret with strangers, but your acquaintances and friends might hear about it more than they want to.

You might be thinking, "I know I have regrets. But this guy says I can live without them. What planet is he on?"

I get it. So let's explore what it means to live without regret.

Regret Is Your Choice

You can choose to live with or without regret. You can choose to make feelings of regret productive or destructive for you and your relationships with others.

Living without regret means you *form* and *perform* plans to minimize the risk of regret. When regret does come, it need not be a chronic state for your life. You can commit to ***transform*** it into a potential-filled, hopeful experience by learning from it.

Forming, performing, and transforming are not easy, but when you practice these disciplines, your thinking changes. When the way you think changes, your emotions change. When your emotions change, your overall attitude and outlook change for the good. This has the potential to change the course of your life.

Living without regret means you choose what you will give your attention to and how much you will give, plan to do it, and do it. What you devote your attention to is an indicator of your values.

Your attention is in great demand. Sights, sounds, sensations, smells, and even tastes, people, opportunities, computer screens, smart phones, pagers, billboards, televisions, food, drink, or something else is at every turn screaming for your attention. But you can only pay attention to so much. If you tried to take everything in, you would be quickly overwhelmed.

We are able to be selective in our attention and we can tune out the uninteresting and unimportant. However, unimportant or marginally important things can crowd out the important and most valuable.

You pay attention to what you value or what demands your attention. For example, when you are driving, I hope you choose to pay attention to the sights, the sounds, the feel of your vehicle, the road, other vehicles, and potential hazards around you. You don't have the mental capacity to pay attention to all of the landmarks, signage, landscape, and movement you pass as you drive. You ignore them completely or bring them quickly into and out of your immediate memory.

As with driving, you can decide whether to give your attention to work, spouse, hobbies, career, financial issues, self-care, leisure, kids, newspaper, home maintenance, or something else. Obviously some things will not get as much attention as others. **To avoid regret, decide what you will give your attention to and how much you will give.** Then plan to do it, and do it.

Living without regret means thinking critically about the deepest things of life. It means examining your beliefs, goals, relationships, the quality and focus of your work, and the legacy you will leave.

This reflective, critical thinking doesn't just happen. If you are a career person, I am sure you think about your job a lot. How about your family? Your health? What you will have to show for your life at the end of it? Such thinking requires the use of your working memory. Just as attention is limited, your working memory is limited. A few years ago we thought our working memory had the capacity to think of about five to seven items at once. Now research indicates the capacity is only about four items at once. So it is important to record your thoughts in some way, be it writing on paper or entering them into your electronic device or memorizing them so you can work with them in the present and access them in the future.

Thinking is hard work. In fact, we know that the brain is the most energy-hungry organ of the body and that the most energy-consuming process is determining priorities. It makes sense, then, that deciding what is most important for the focus of your working memory is tiring.

Those who are in high-stress, high-demand, high-income jobs are highly focused on their work. They can afford to pay their bills but are often delinquent in paying them just because they do not have the capacity to think about their job and personal business. They are not paying attention to or thinking critically about much other than their work. They can be surprised when they lose their families, other relationships, and even their health.

I've identified three simple ingredients necessary for living without regret:

1. Form: Thoughtful Planning

> *If you fail to plan, you plan to fail.*
> —Winston Churchill

Living without regret involves thoughtful planning. This is a critical thinking process that involves creativity, the ability to solve problems, and, more important, clearly identifying the problem first of all. Being proactive in this way is one of the most sensible ways to avoid regret.

When you travel, it makes sense to plan your destination, route, and any stopovers you want to make. The same is true in life. Plan where you want to end, and determine the route you want to take in getting there and what landmarks you will need to see. Some get this backward; they get in motion without sufficient planning.

People are always amazed at how much simpler it is to make decisions when they have the ultimate goal set and they have their focus on that goal instead of all the other sensory noise around them.

2. Perform: Take Action

Without action, there is no traction.
—Anonymous

Living without regret involves action. You can make the most thoughtful plan in the world, but unless you commit to the plan and take action on it, you can experience feelings of regret and failure. Think about the New Year's resolutions you've made that you abandoned within a couple of weeks.

Planning can be fun. Action can be scary. But we learn in action. If we are not acting, we are likely not learning. So once your thoughtful plan is in place, take action. Start with baby steps. When taken together, those baby steps become giant steps.

3. Transform: Live in the Present

Many of us crucify ourselves between two thieves—
regret for the past and fear of the future.
—Fulton Oursler

Living without regret involves learning from the past, focusing on the present, and glancing at the future. Regret is always about the past, which can no longer be influenced by you. As you move through life you can feel sorrow, remorse, disappointment, or a sense of loss related to a word, a fault, or an action in the past. It's a part of being human.

But you need not live with the regret of the past. Regret can cause you to miss the present and walk lamely into the future. You can sacrifice the present and future on the altar of the past. Use the experiences of the past to learn how to live better in the present and for the future.

Mindfully live in the present while planning for the future. Avoid focusing on the future at the expense of the present moment. If you are over-focused on the next goal, you can miss an important present-moment learning point that affects that next goal.

Attitude

Through planning and taking action on my plans, I have managed to avoid a lot of regret. Through observation and reflection, I have also managed to avoid a lot of the regret I see others experiencing. I have found that living without regret involves an attitude that whatever may come, I will find something to learn from it and use what is learned to move toward my purpose.

Rather than wallowing in guilt, shame, and remorse, I cultivate an attitude of wonder and curiosity, and I know that I am always in progress. Though experiences may be difficult, they are not regrettable. Adjusting my attitude is never easy and never quick, but I know I cannot reach my potential, achieve my purpose, or live to the fullest without time in the crucible of challenging life experiences.

I was sitting in the office of a university official who knew some of my experiences quite well. Out of the blue he said, "You know, you're amazingly healthy for what you've been through." My response to him was: "I appreciate the thought. I believe I am healthy because I have tried to take what I have experienced and find meaning in it. I want it to be useful for my life."

I am a professor, and I include this quote by Charles Swindoll in my syllabus every semester:

The longer I live, the more I realize the impact of attitude on life. Attitude, to me, is more important than facts. It is more important than the past, the education, the money, than circumstances, than failure, than successes, than what other people think or say or do. It is more important than appearance, giftedness or skill. It will make or break a company... a church... a home. The remarkable thing is we have a choice every day regarding the attitude we will embrace for that day. We cannot change our past... we cannot change the fact that people will act in a certain way. We cannot change the inevitable. The only thing we can do is play on the one string we have, and that is our attitude. I am convinced that life is 10% what happens to me and 90% of how I react to it. And so it is with you. We are in charge of our attitudes.

I have noticed that some of the most in-touch, deep, and wise individuals have been through some pretty challenging trials. But they don't whine about them. They adopt a learner's attitude and grow from the experience. You can do this also and live without regret.

No Armchair Quarterback

Keep in mind that we often use others' words for emotions of regret. We might say we feel:

Sorry

Disappointed

Heartbroken

Or we might express regret by saying:

I hate that...

I wish that...

I've experienced emotions of regret more often than I want to and for many of the same reasons you have—failure; broken relationships; health issues with myself, my family, or friends; and hurtful words and actions directed at me, my family, or friends. I'm not special, and want you to know that I'm not an armchair quarterback telling you what to do from the sidelines. I'm in the fray with you.

I continue to commit the time and do the hard work of forming, performing, and transforming to live without regret. But if you asked me if I live without regret today, I'd tell you, "Indeed!" I use the principles in this book (and more) all the time.

Recently a client said to me, "I wonder how things would be if I had known ten years ago what I know now?" This has a tone of regret in it. With this client, I don't think the problem was lack of trying. I do believe he was working with all the light he had, and that's all one can do. I encouraged him to start from where he is now and be responsible for what he now knows.

What about you? You are about to know more about how to avoid regret. You need not look back and wonder. Plan and take action with the light you are about to receive to experience a life without regret.

Faith Sticky Note: **A Bigger Picture**

Living without regret requires trust that I have been created for a purpose that is bigger than my circumstances and even my life itself. I believe God has a purpose for me. It's the purpose for which I was created and is a perfect fit for me. When I live in alignment with this purpose, I experience fulfillment, joy, abundance, and meaning. Pursuing another plan is like wearing shoes that don't fit—the journey is long, painful, and filled with feelings of regret.

When I am moving in line with this purpose, I create a zone of freedom in which I can choose from a variety of options, and God is okay with whatever I choose. Sometimes my choices work out well, and sometimes not so well. Sometimes events happen that are out of my control. When the consequences are unpleasant, God takes them and fashions them for a good outcome. He is continually at work, using life experiences, pleasant and unpleasant, as tools to teach me and make me be more like Christ.

In the difficult circumstances of life I find great hope in my belief that God is with me, always pursuing me as a partner in his enterprise, teaching me, and using "all things" to help me be more like what He wants me to be. This is a part of my belief system—the way I make sense of life—and it gives me a plan for living without regret.

FORM: Planning to Avoid Regret

"How do I fit in all this?" "What's my place?" "Which way do I go?" "What's my path?" "Who am I and why am I here?"

Unfortunately the great majority of people don't find clear answers to these questions soon enough. They jump into life's river head first. They never consider whether it might be better to walk, run, crawl, ride, or fly instead of swim. They have little idea whether or not they are moving in the right direction, where they will end the journey, or how they will end it. **They are on a poorly planned, high-risk journey that is sure to be filled with regret.**

Then when they have little or no time left, they slow down, only to regret that they allowed life to carry them along. They regret that they never intentionally worked toward a purpose, vision, and legacy that would have lived on powerfully beyond their grave.

Planning to live without regret requires digging deep to get to the real you and what you really want. In the chapters in this section you will be challenged to create a crystal-clear:

- Definition of self—positively define who you are and simultaneously say who you are not
- Identification of your most important values
- Connection to your vocation, or calling
- Written personal mission statement specific enough to guide you but not restrict you
- Personal vision statement
- Statement of broad guiding principles for interaction with others

Chapter 3

Who Am I? Clearly Define the Unique You

I will give thanks to You, for I am fearfully and wonderfully made;
Wonderful are Your works, And my soul knows it very well.

—Psalm 139:14 (NASB95)

There are no two people exactly alike. Some of our differences are products of nature, designed by our genetic code. Others are products of how we were nurtured—of the instruction and example of our parents, teachers, and life experiences.

We seek training to help us develop talents and abilities for which we have some natural inclination. Some abilities for which we do not have sufficient natural inclination can be developed with hard work and practice.

For example, I have extensive training in playing the piano, but no natural gift for it. As a result I had to work hard to squeak by my piano requirements while working toward my undergraduate degree in music. Some fellow students, though they worked hard as well, seemed to come by it far more naturally.

Our differences make us unique, one-of-a-kind people.

We Love the Familiar

Our similarities provide common ground for relating to and understanding one another. We are more comfortable with those who look, talk, think, and act like us. Personal styles, opinions, preferences, and belief systems of others that are familiar to us are less confusing, less disturbing, and allow for less effort when developing a relationship. We want others to be more like us and they want us to be more like them. We sometimes try to manipulate or pressure others into being like us because we love the familiar.

But we are also uniquely different from one another. When we live true to who we are, those differences create possibilities for both novel contributions and relationship challenges.

Differences put us on guard. We react to differences and unexpected changes as if they are threats. This is a function of our reactive, protective, reptilian brains. Sometimes the reaction is only a sense of discomfort. At other times, depending on the degree of difference, we have a more dramatic reaction that prompts our sympathetic nervous system into action. Our adrenalin flows and our body prepares for fight, flight, or freeze.

We can't live in a constant state of being on guard, so we try to lower this anxiety by adjusting our thinking to create greater understanding and comfort. For example, let's say you drive home, get out of your car, secure it, go into your house, get a good night's sleep, and when you go to your car the next morning, the doors and the trunk are open. This is different from what you expected, and immediately you are on guard. You begin to think aloud as you investigate the situation, trying to gain an understanding of what has happened, only to discover that a family member was looking for something in the car, was distracted, and left all the doors open.

Our reactions to differences have a big impact on the way we relate to various personalities and styles. Some differences don't fit our understanding of a normal personality or an acceptable style, so we need a category in which to place them. Our tendency is to take the easy way out and group them with others (stereotyping), make biased assumptions, label differences as "weird," judge them, marginalize them, and warn others to beware of them. We talk about them to others who are like us, trying to gain assurance that our thinking is right. Our processes may be very emotional, reactive, and irrational (not thinking).

For example, at a gathering you're attending, one person in the room is more outgoing than you or more direct and frank than you are comfortable with as they talk with you. Depending on the degree of difference, you can sense anything from discomfort to a full flight, fight, or freeze reaction. You might label that person as boisterous or obnoxious. You might share your opinion with others. You might retreat to the corner of the room. Or you can lower your anxiety by breathing deeply, relaxing, and recognizing that they don't know your personality, are not on the attack, and this is just their way of trying to relate to you.

We have these reactions to others and they have them toward us. Such reactions toward us can lead to our trying harder to fit in if we have not yet gained a clear sense of our uniqueness and appreciation for it. This compromise can be a cause of regret.

There are a few different ways we attempt to fit in with the crowd:

Temporary and Voluntary
Sometimes we need to make a voluntary, temporary adjustment in order to live in community and work well with others. An example is when we need to communicate with another person in their native language.

Needy
When we desperately want to fit in with a group or society, we might try to behave like someone else altogether, believing that borrowed behavior is more desirable than our own unique behavior would be. Thus we betray our own uniqueness to fit in.

Pressured to Fit
Sometimes we allow others to pressure us into behaving a certain way. We allow *them* to determine who we are to be and how we are to act. As we allow this influence to have its way, we learn to be helpless for doing anything about it. In *Becoming Your Best: A Self-Help Guide for Thinking People*, Ronald Richardson notes that living according to self-chosen principles instead of those chosen by someone else is essential to emotional maturity, moral excellence, and firmness. Those who live according to self-chosen principles tend to experience a happier, more satisfied life, with healthier relationships.[2]

Knowing and being your unique, authentic self takes hard work and great courage. You will be loved by some and hated by others. Since you're reading this book, living your life with integrity—being who you really are, inside and out—probably matters to you.

Going with the Flow
Some of us float along with whatever thinking and behavior seems to work in the moment; we simply have not chosen to invest the time and energy needed to explore, define, celebrate, and commit to our uniqueness.

Living in Integrity

When your way of acting is consistent with the unique qualities inside you and your belief system, you are living in integrity. The word comes from Latin, meaning "whole." A person with integrity is whole, undivided, uncompromised. Living in integrity can be inconvenient and difficult, and we often choose instead to conform to the behavior of others around us instead of living true to our real selves.

Once you clearly identify your strengths, character, style, purpose, values, and vision, you are more ready to live an undivided life; it's not easy, but you are more ready. When you stand for who you are and let others do the same, you are far more likely to avoid feelings of regret.

The opposite of integrity is hypocrisy, which comes from the Greek word that means an actor or one who pretends to be what he is not.

If you are a *Star Wars* fan, you will remember when Obi Wan and young Anakin Skywalker encountered a "changeling" who frequently changed in appearance in order to disguise herself, blend in with and relate to those around her, and elude her pursuers. But when she was dying, she could not hold up the front and reverted to her natural form. When a person is not living in integrity, they're like the changeling—always changing to fit in and keep people from seeing who they are really and naturally. They live according to the expectations of others rather than their own purpose and values. What you see and relate to on the outside constantly changes. Changelings are plagued with inner conflict.

But you can take uniqueness to extremes. There are those who believe their self-chosen way is the only way and every other way of being and doing is wrong. Sometimes they cut themselves off from everyone else or try to force others to fit their mold. One way or the other, they alienate themselves from others and have a very lonely existence. **Take courage, be you, and let others be themselves.**

Without Regret in Uniqueness

You create a giant opportunity for regret when you give in to the pressure to be like someone else and fail to recognize, value, and live as your unique self—and when you pressure others to be more like you. When you look back on your life, you might discover that you lived according to someone else's definition of *self-created* and you never risked being yourself. By then time will be short for adjustment, but **it's never too late to do away with regret and be uniquely you.**

Discovering the Unique

I asked John, a forty-five-year-old client of mine, "What would you like to coach around this week?" After a moment of silence he started to laugh and speak at the same time. He said, "You know, during the last year I've learned that I likely have ADHD and that I am really much more introverted than extroverted! How do you get to my age and not know these things?" What followed was one of the most exciting periods of discovery by a client in my coaching career. His voice gained energy, he held more conviction, and he expressed excitement as if having discovered a whole new way of living. And he had. I barely said a paragraph's worth of words during his self-discovery.

John is extremely intelligent and perceptive, and loves people. He had always been a little confused about who he was and how he should show up in his day-to-day interactions with family, coworkers, church friends, and others. His mentor is more extroverted than he is (John thinks), so John thought that was the way a successful practitioner in his field was to be. John's discomfort with trying to be this way was a mystery to him, and he was often out of energy.

In his breakthrough session, John crystallized his discovery that it was okay to be just who he is — more introverted than his mentor. He will make his greatest contribution to his family, work, and the world by doing this.

TAKE ACTION: Affirm to yourself that you are valuable, competent, and capable in your uniqueness. Don't spend your life trying to be someone you are not. Get out of the box of others' expectations. Their discomfort with your uniqueness says more about them than it does about you. Their discomfort does not make you wrong.

Faith Sticky Note: Uniquely Made

If another scientific discovery was never made, the variety of God's creations is already beyond comprehension. Yet scientists are discovering new species of life and more about known species all the time. Many of these discoveries reveal jaw-dropping beauty, value to the environment, and uniqueness across species and among species.

The human brain is also beyond imagination. A single neuron connects to hundreds to thousands of synapses. The brain has an average of 100 billion neurons and an estimated .15 quadrillion synapses in the cortex.[3] There are more potential connections between neurons than there are atoms in the universe.[4]

These connections can be different for every person depending on their nature and how they were nurtured. Think about what this means about the number of possibilities for uniqueness we have.

All these discoveries and potential for differences further convince me that God created me uniquely. I am "fearfully and wonderfully made" to fulfill His calling to be exactly as I am.

Chapter 4

Who Am I? How Am I Unique?

It is of practical value to learn to like yourself.
Since you must spend so much time with yourself
you might as well get some satisfaction out of the relationship.

—*Norman Vincent Peale*

We each have so many valuable, unique qualities that they can't be counted. But we often compromise, starve, discount, and lack awareness about our particular strengths, interests, gifts, talents, personality, style, and experience.

It's essential to identify and embrace your unique qualities if you want to live fully, meaningfully, and without regret.

Your Unique Strengths

A strength is a capacity, natural or developed, to do a particular thing better than you do other things. When you work within your strengths, you are your most productive self. Strengths are different from person to person, so it's important to identify your own unique strengths, develop them, and work inside them. It would be truly regrettable to live without capitalizing on your strengths or to try to mimic others using only your weaknesses.

Identify, Develop, and Work within Your Strengths
You can identify your strengths through the use of assessments. There are plenty of assessments available to get you started, such as the Birkman® method or Strengthsfinder®.

Another way to identify strengths is to examine your aptitude, your inclinations, and your powerful leanings. What seems to come easily to you? That's probably a natural strength. What things do you do that seem to make a big contribution? Those are probably strengths, too. Look at the qualities you have that people typically call strengths, such as intellect or a winsome public persona. Don't stop there. Look for qualities that people might not readily identify as strengths, such as the ability to reflect on multiple aspects of a problem, a practical manual skillfulness, or an ability to quickly create order from disorder. Look for strengths—both typical ones and those that seem outside the box—that are uniquely yours.

Focus on developing your strengths rather than improving your weaknesses. For example, I am weak at performing some manual tasks, and I do not try to improve on that. I get someone else to do manual tasks for me in most cases. I am not good at math and I don't plan on taking any training to improve that; I would rather employ an accountant. Spending the rest of your life working on weaknesses will yield very little and sabotage any possibility of achieving your potential effect on the world. If the weakness doesn't hurt you or anyone else, or won't cost you your job or relationships, ignore it and live with it. Instead, develop your strengths to their maximum potential.

Give attention to weaknesses only when they are fatal flaws that hurt you or others, or when they get in the way of achieving what you need or want. Author and consultant Jack Zenger recommends working on your strengths only when such "fatal flaws" are improved.[5] If you have a profound weakness such as an inability to perform required tasks, an inability to order your life so you can excel, or an inability to be socially skillful, work on it. If you have a moral weakness that hurts you or others, work on it. Otherwise, work on your strengths.

Individuals who are powerful communicators, dynamic visionaries, fierce competitors, outstanding leaders, or profoundly creative, sometimes, by their own admission, cannot organize their way out of a sack. Are they weak? Absolutely not! I encourage them to continue working within their strengths and to bring a person alongside them whose strength and passion is organization. I encourage them to delegate to others those tasks that fall outside the scope of their strengths, and forget about it. My mantra is: **Do what you do best and what uniquely only you can do.** Use your strengths and supplement your weaknesses by teaming with those who are strong where you are weak.

Look for jobs or tasks that are an excellent fit for the strengths you identify. Open your mind and ask, "What would it be like to work within my strengths 90 percent of the time?" Envision it and work toward it. This begins with finding or creating opportunities (jobs and task requirements) that are the right fit for your strengths. Don't take any old job just because it's available or it pays well; you will be the one who gets stuck and ends up paying. Know your strengths, communicate them well and with confidence, and find a job that fits. If you are already in a job, maneuver for a higher percentage of strengths-related work each day. You will likely be more productive and happy in your work.

When overused, strengths can become weaknesses. Work within your strengths, but don't blow the top off. Some people are great analysts, able to see details other don't see. But taken to the extreme this strength can slow or stop the analyst in making decisions. And those who are very task-oriented know the feeling of taking on way too many projects at once—even when they are good at them.

Your Unique Interests

Unfortunately we can get so deeply involved in what we "have" to do that we completely lose connection with what we *love* to do. The things we deeply enjoy doing get crowded out of our minds and our schedules, but not our hearts. As a result we experience an ill-defined discontent and a longing for more—and this can lead to regret.

Whatever your unique interests may be, it is important that your job and your life in general allow you to invest your energy in those areas. You can invest your energy in attaining financial, social, or political security, but this can ultimately feel very empty. **When you tune in to your most powerful interests, you can gain a sense of great fulfillment and joy.** Choose work that allows you to work within your area of interest most of the time. Life is too short to work in a job in which your interest is low.

Your talents and interests may lie where you find "flow." Author Mihaly Csikszentmihalyi describes flow as an optimal experience in which individuals report feelings of concentration and deep enjoyment. It is a state of concentration so focused that the individual is absolutely absorbed in the activity. In flow, you feel strong, alert, in effortless control, unselfconscious, and at the peak of your abilities. You experience flow when activities absorb you so much that time seems to stand still, emotional problems disappear, and there is a feeling of exhilaration. What engages and fits you so completely that when you are involved in it, you feel satisfied and fulfilled?

My client Ron is the CEO of a very successful business. He skeptically entered into coaching after being encouraged by a friend and coworker. The key question we focused on was "What do you love doing?" He liked his job, but he *loved* connecting people with resources. Fortunately his job allowed him to intentionally incorporate what he loved into his day-to-day responsibilities, and this helped him love his job even more. Now he is more intentional about doing the thing he loves to benefit customers, employees, and coworkers.

Your Unique Talents

You have talents that are unique to those of others. If you say, "I play the piano, but lots of people do that," I'll tell you, "Nobody does it like you." Your talents are unique only to you. We are all uniquely and variously intelligent, talented, and gifted for making a difference in the world around us. No one can do exactly what you do in the way you do it.

Unfortunately, in our efforts to fit in, we sometimes discount our talents and gifts by comparing them to others', soft-pedaling them, or hiding them. Even the most gifted and talented among us can be insecure and question the quality of their talent and their contribution to the world even though they are famous.

Your Unique Personality

The fact that you have more of or less of some quality than other people do makes you unique. Undue comparison to others discourages and limits you. See yourself as complete, whole, capable, and competent just as you are.

In her book *Quiet: The Power of Introverts in a World that Can' t Stop Talking*, author Susan Cain notes that the word *personality* did not even exist until the eighteenth century. The idea of having a "good personality" was not widely engaged until the twentieth century. Cain carefully studied aspects of cultural history in America that led to the rise of extroversion or outgoingness as the preferred normal ("the extrovert ideal") and introversion as a less-than-desirable personality trait.

Cain says that because of this social milieu, many who are introverted try to live in a more extroverted fashion than is true to their native personality, or retreat in social settings believing they have little to contribute and don't fit in.[6] Not advisable. Remember my client John from the last chapter?

Some try to explain away repulsive, unproductive, mean, rude, or disrespectful behavior by saying, "Well, that's just my personality" or "That's just the way I am." But these are not basic, unique, helpful personality traits. They reflect bad habits, poor character, and social insensitivity. If these belong to you, enlist a strong, honest, safe accountability partner, a therapist, a coach, or all of the above to help you be happier in life. If you are the object of such behavior, be sure to read the chapters on defining your relationships with others, boundaries, and assertiveness.

TAKE ACTION: Learn to love and respect your personality. **Make a list of 100 things you appreciate about your personality.** Identify those unique aspects of yourself that make a real contribution and build others up. Embrace them, protect them, nurture them, and capitalize on them to make a difference in the world.

Unique Styles of Relating

Because each of our personalities is different and we have been nurtured in different ways, we each have a unique style of relating to others.

Mary loved ideas and change but did not readily put structure into her ideas. Mary's strength lay in coming up with visionary ideas and persuading people to buy into them.

Jana, Mary's supervisor, preferred consistency, order, and structure. Jana's strength was in organization and administration.

Excited, Mary brought her ideas to Jana. Jana's first question was usually "How will this be organized and managed?" Mary got frustrated, seeing Jana's response as impatience and lack of appreciation for the idea itself and Mary's work. Mary wondered if Jana believed her performance was not up to par. Though very respectful of one another, both were frustrated.

I had Mary and Jana, along with sixteen others in their organization, complete a Birkman® assessment. As I reviewed the data, I commented to the CEO that their personalities and styles were very different and they might enjoy some coaching. At the end of a coaching session with me, Mary said, "One big thing that I came to understand is that Jana is just different than me. She's not mad at me, or trying to control me, she just sees and thinks about things differently." Mary moved to another job that capitalized on her strengths and engaged her deepest interests and personality. Jana decided that she preferred doing her old job that did not require as much supervision. Both are much happier.

Your Unique Experience

We each have a unique experience of life and the world. Many influences mold and affect our experience. Some help us function at higher levels and others seem to inhibit our functioning and can lead to greater dysfunction. Some of the influences that create our experience of life and the world include:

- Relationships (parents, family, other authority figures, peers, acquaintances, strangers, enemies)
- History (what happened at particular times in our life)
- Words spoken to us (encouraging, discouraging, positive, negative, building, breaking)
- Capabilities (sensory, motor skills, ability to think)
- Culture and cultural change
- Religious and spiritual influences
- Our actions, their efficacy, and their consequences (good or ill)
- Information encountered and discovered
- Our own genetic makeup
- Health
- Education

Whether you have had a wonderful life experience or one that you believe was not so wonderful, you can capitalize on the experience. How you embrace it makes you who you are and who you are to become. I recently read a great follow-up to that popular yet fatalistic statement: "It is what it is." The follow-up is: "Now what matters is what you learn from it and make of it for the future."

Your unique life experience has equipped you for making a contribution that no one else can. Embrace it and use every ounce of it to your advantage for the realization of your potential and making a unique contribution.

My son Jonathan is a highly intelligent, imaginative, and creative individual of whom I am extremely proud. He is hard-working, respectful of others, and has a deep faith. He is unique in all the ways described above.

During his childhood and adolescent years, his uniqueness flowered and he was, at times, misunderstood by others. Sometimes our family did not understand why others responded to him as they did. We accepted him unconditionally. When he was in middle school he told us, "I've decided to be who I am even if others don't like me."

During my wife's many years as a school teacher and my many years in youth ministry, we saw many well-meaning parents force their children into molds that didn't honor their children's personalities. The result was often dysfunction, rebellion, and/or the child not realizing their potential.

We parented in light of this general belief: "As long as it is not morally wrong, spiritually hurtful, or dangerous to others, and it won't do serious physical harm to our child, let him spread his wings." Believe me, this was a big choice for us since we both have pretty strong convictions about behavior and social interaction as they affect others.

We determined that we would bless our son's uniqueness and allow as much of his individuality to come forth as was reasonable and socially practical. We would not try to put him in a box or force him into the expectations of others.

Today my friends tell me that they admire the fact that we always let Jonathan be Jonathan. One of his college music professors told me that my son is one of the most creative individuals he has ever known, and he said, "When he comes into my office, I hold on to my chair because I know very soon the creative conversations will be flying over my head."

I'm glad we didn't try to make him someone he wasn't.

Faith Sticky Note: Managing the Unique

I believe God owns it all—time, money, material objects, talents, giftedness, skills, the air we breathe, the beats of our heart; we have no resources of our own. God entrusts me with management of certain things—some unique to me—and I am a caretaker. He expects me to manage His things in ways that honor Him and achieve His purposes, and I get to enjoy them in the process. God entrusts more to some than to others, but all are equally responsible for the care of that which is entrusted to them.

When I view my unique strengths, giftedness, abilities, and relationships as belonging to God, it makes all the difference in how I care for them and use them.

Because no one is exactly like me, no one else can make the contribution I can make. There are roles and responsibilities that only my unique self can fulfill. If I don't fulfill these with integrity, they won't get done to the fullness of their potential.

No one can make the exact contribution you can make as your unique self. Our unique contributions are needed in this world.

What's yours?

Chapter 5

Where Am I Going?

Don't it always seem to go
That you don't know what you've got
Till it's gone
—Joni Mitchell

You need do very little to reach the end of life, sooner or later. The question is "Will you have mattered?" You decide what the answer is. You can simply allow the breezes, currents, winds, and waves of your days to carry you along until you come to the end. You can allow people's expectations, opinions, approval, and rejection to direct your course. Or you can adopt your own principles that allow you to be more, see more, and achieve more that really matters.

Your Values

Values are our beliefs about what is most important to us. *Valuables* are things that are important to us and reflect our values. Your sense of self, vocation, mission, and vision grows out of your values.

You can be living by a set of values even though you haven't clearly identified them. If you haven't identified them, trivial, selfish, and immediate things seem more important than your values and what's truly valuable to you does not get the attention it needs and deserves.

Some of us have considered our values but are not yet clear about our top values—too many things seem to be of equal value. If I asked you to state your top five values, could you do it?

So many successful professionals have lives that are on the rocks—failed marriages, broken relationships with children, lost friendships, slippery ethics, and general misery. They weren't clear enough about their values to intentionally nurture them and commit to them. Now they grieve the loss.

Make decisions about values now, before you discover in hindsight what was really valuable to you. For an exercise that will help you develop greater clarity about your values, go to www.DiscoverYourTrueCourse.com/readerbonus and download your free Values Exercise. You can work through this exercise on your own. A coach, however, can assist you in working through it more surely and completely. Don't wait until something you value is gone due to lack of attention and you are plagued by regret.

Your Sense of Vocation

Your sense of vocation informs your mission. Your vocation is not your occupation or profession; it is an umbrella under which you live all of life, including your occupation.

The English word *vocation* comes from the Latin *vocare,* which means "to call." We have reduced *vocation* to refer to endeavors in life such as your occupation that are not nearly as high and noble as your vocation. A *calling* or sense of "call" comes from a higher source outside yourself and beyond human sources. It is an invitation to be involved in something much bigger than you and your world.

You may have an occupation, but it will quickly seem mundane and feelings of disappointment will arise unless you have a *vocation* to which your occupation is related. **You need something nobler, higher, and more enduring—a calling on which to build a life that makes a difference and is without regret.**

Your Purpose, Mission, Direction

Alice: Would you tell me, please, which way I ought to go from here?
The Cat: That depends a good deal on where you want to get to.
Alice: I don't much care where.
The Cat: Then it doesn't much matter which way you go.
Alice: ...so long as I get somewhere.
The Cat: Oh, you're sure to do that, if only you walk long enough.

—Lewis Carroll, Through the Looking Glass

Isn't it interesting how we don't practice the things that make sense, like deciding where we are going before we start down the road? Some of us are satisfied having no real direction and being moved by whatever current of life comes our way. Unfortunately, one of those currents might be what another person told us we should do. Or, like Alice, we keep hoping we will run up on "somewhere" and that when we do, we will have achieved and experienced joy, success, and fulfillment. A good outcome from this practice is not likely. We get "somewhere," but it's likely not where we want to be, and we will likely experience regret.

TAKE ACTION: Written Personal Mission Statement

A clear, written personal mission statement provides a self-chosen, overarching guide for determining your best actions and next steps for reaching your ultimate destination—your purpose. Such a statement grows out of your beliefs about who you are and why you are here in this place at this time. **A written personal mission statement is essential to living a life without regret.**

Your mission statement is more stable and enduring than a list of goals, and embodies what you powerfully believe must be the focus of your life. Goals are important and contribute to the fulfillment of your mission, but they come and go. If your goals do not fit under the umbrella of your mission statement, they are not your best goals.

I believe both purpose and vision as defined in this book are involved in "the dream" defined by Daniel Levinson, an adult development researcher who wrote *The Seasons of a Man's Life* and *The Seasons of a Woman's Life*. Levinson found that the dream is developed in early adulthood. It includes one's goals and aspirations and is an idealized fantasy that pictures oneself projected into the future. A powerful dream gives a person energy—a sense of destiny and courage—for moving forward purposefully. Men often develop the dream around their careers. The dream for women leans toward relationships and family. (This does not discount the interest of women in career pursuits, but they often choose an earlier or later time in their lives to pursue a career.)[7]

Purpose and vision give us a guide for our lives as well as a way to evaluate how we are doing at various transition points in middle and late adulthood. Levinson refers to these transitions points as crisis periods in life, referring to times in our lives when adjustments must be made. While unsettling, these periods need not be times of panic. According to Levinson, these crises develop based on how our current life structure is reflecting our "dream" and how it might need to be adjusted.

I've found that people run the gamut when it comes to writing personal mission statements.

- Some are clear about their business mission but are unclear about their personal mission.
- Some have read about creating a personal mission statement but have done nothing with the information.
- Some are too busy to establish direction by creating a personal mission statement.
- Some have developed a personal mission statement for a seminar or class assignment but not sufficiently for it to benefit them.
- Some have a written a personal mission statement and occasionally think about it.
- And a very few have a clearly written personal mission statement and live it.

I have asked many people if they have a personal mission statement, and the only one who had written one on his own was my son Jonathan. When I asked him what it was, he quoted it. And he lives it. His example challenged me to faithfully review my own personal mission statement, keep a clear focus on it, and live it out consistently.

My client Bill told me, "I developed a mission statement before, but working through this with a coach has really helped me get clearer about it and put it into action. It comes to my mind during the day and helps me make decisions to keep my life on track."

Why It Is Important
A written personal mission statement is important for several reasons. It can:

- Take you out of an aimless existence
- Provide a tool for deciding between the "good" and the "best" in your life
- Give you a sense of energy for living
- Provide an empowering focus for your life
- Provide an intangible sense of confidence

- Provide an anchor point to prevent being driven off course in times of uncertainty
- Assist with priority management

Subsequent to the development of their personal mission statement, I hear people enthusiastically refer to it as their guide for making decisions and refining their leadership in their careers and in their families.

In the course of his coaching with me, Jose had developed a written personal mission statement. One day he called and said, "Can you come by my office? I need to visit with you a little."

He seemed a little troubled as he began to tell me about a decision he needed to make in the next twenty-four hours. There was to be a birth in his extended close family very soon. Jose was trying to decide whether to stay in town for the weekend or take a trip out of town. He could see that both options were very desirable but was divided in his thoughts because, even though the baby was expected soon, who could really know when the baby would come? I listened deeply and then asked simply, "What does your mission statement say?"

There was a marked silence followed by, "Oh. If I follow my mission statement I will stay here since family is my highest priority." Decision made. As it turned out, the baby was born that weekend. The decision he made was unregrettable.

The work Jose had done in developing his foundational definition of self, values, vocation, mission, and vision helped his decision-making be clear and less anxiety-filled. The time he'd invested was well worth his effort.

Tools for Developing a Written Personal Mission Statement
There are a number of tools and exercises that can help you develop your personal mission statement. Among these are:
- Religious or other writings that inspire you
- Paper and pencil. There is something about the tactile experience of putting pencil to paper that makes things click.
- An exercise at www.DiscoverYourTrueCourse.com/readerbonus—download your free Mission Statement Development Exercise.
- A coach. The safe, supportive, challenging environment of a coaching

relationship can help you get past the negative thinking, create a fresh dream for the rest of your life, and start moving toward it today. A number of people tell me that coaching has been essential in their success.

- Exercise: Identify five individuals, living or deceased, whom you respect and admire. Write down why you admire them. This offers clues to your values and mission.
- Exercise: Write your epitaph or obituary.
- Exercise: Imagine people walking by your casket and speaking about you. What would you like them to say? Consider individually what you would like your spouse, children, friends, and coworkers to say.
- Exercise: Identify your personal uniqueness. Your personal mission statement can be an expression of this uniqueness.

Write It Down

It's so important to let your ideas about your personal mission statement come out of your mind and then record them in writing. With everything else swirling around in your brain, ideas about purpose can be fragmented, obscured, or lost entirely. So write them down.

Personal Vision

A personal vision is a snapshot of your preferred future and expresses what things will look like at a particular point in time if you are faithful to your purpose. Your personal vision is related to your personal mission statement, but they are not the same thing.

Once you get clear about your definition of self, values, vocation, and mission, it's time to identify your personal vision in all its clarity and expansiveness. A vision must be big to be effective. It must challenge the imagination and evoke an emotional response of inspiration.

You can develop multiple vision statements over the course of your life that mark the way to completing your purpose. Sometimes you need to adjust your vision and refocus. A fresh vision can bring a renewed sense of purpose and inspire the energy and the courage to move toward it.

You can identify a vision for your life by keeping your definition of self, values, vocation, and mission in mind and then dreaming big—bodaciously big. Put every big, seemingly unrealistic thing that comes to mind on paper. Don't think about "how"; just think about "what" and "who." Try dreaming about what could be with no financial, time, or other restrictions.

If this sounds outlandish to you or it is hard for you to imagine how to do this, it is likely because you have either forgotten how to do it or you were not allowed to do it earlier in your life. As a child you did this naturally, but along the way an especially realistic, fearful, or judgmental individual(s) probably told you that your visionary, dreamy ideas were stupid, unrealistic, impossible, impractical, silly, crazy, nonsensical, or lacked common sense. You stopped imagining what could be and limited yourself to what was acceptable to others. Silence those voices. Learn to dream again.

As you begin vision development now, you may run up against resistance from:

- Your own judgments
- Your own sense of inadequacy
- The discouraging voices of others
- Your fear
- Your limiting beliefs (such as "It's too late!" "I'm too old." "I can't.")

Avoid judging your thoughts as crazy, stupid, or impractical.

A case in point might be Alan's vision. He is in the early stages of his career and his family is young. Alan has a personal vision of becoming financially independent, being free not to work, caring for his children but not spoiling them, and endowing a foundation to address the need for clean water in Africa. He is not yet clear about how this can come to pass, but this is his vision.

If you look at Alan's vision with skepticism or it takes your breath away, that's a good sign that it's bodacious. Some might naysay, judge, or caution; they can't relate to dreaming like this. And believe me, it takes Alan's breath away, too.

In the envisioning process, close your eyes and imagine how it will look, feel to your touch, feel in your emotions, taste, smell, and sound when you are in the midst of the vision realized. Write this out or create a visual representation of it and post it where you can see it often.

In their book *Switch: How to Change Things When Change Is Hard*,

Chip and Dan Heath encourage the development of "post cards," which are pictures of points along the way to the achievement of the vision. In Alan's vision, a post card might picture achieving a certain credential that would increase his income. Another might be achieving a certain amount of business in the next five years to put him on track for his big vision. Post cards encourage, keep interest alive, help maintain focus, and create opportunities for celebration and enjoyment on the journey.

Create your personal vision and post cards. Then start walking toward your vision as if it is reality now.

Once you have a clear definition of your self, values, vocation, mission, and vision, you can involve your family in doing the same for themselves individually and as a family. When approached in an age-appropriate way, this can help make life, individually and together, more focused and purposeful and less like a cyclone. It can help couples experience greater harmony and have a bigger impact on the world. It can help teenagers and college students make truly great decisions for their daily living and the future. **When you make this exercise a habit of life, you are certainly planning and acting to live without regret.**

Faith Sticky Note: My Values, Vocation, Mission Statement, and Vision

God's call to each of us is that we be representatives and reflections of Christ in this world in the totality of our being and doing. This is the calling I have accepted. Some accept it and some do not. Though Christians have one vocation, they may have many occupations, with clergy being one among many. All Christians have equal responsibility for living out this vocation.

My top personal values are:
- Relationship to God
- Family
- Love
- Learning
- Excellence
- Influence/Impact

Here is my personal mission statement, which grows out of my sense of vocation and my values:

I believe I am here to glorify God and express my love for Him and others through consistent personal growth in Christ-likeness and facilitating the personal growth in Christ-likeness of others, especially leaders, to the degree that they become consistently multiplying leaders in God's kingdom. I will do this by living a life that reflects Christ and exemplifies the process of continuing learning and multiplying as a Christian leader. I will lovingly invest in the lives of others, assisting them to develop to the fullness of their potential. I will exercise excellence in administration, leadership, effective communication, coaching, mentoring, and preparation and delivery of formal teaching and training. I will do all that is possible so far as it concerns me to develop and maintain healthy relationships and will creatively, proactively address interpersonal problems and conflicts as they may surface. This all begins with my home and family.

Here's my definition of vision from my faith perspective: "A vision is a goal or dream given by God that is so big only He can make it happen." A vision smaller than this represents something I can do on my own without God's work, and as such is not of faith.

My vision for my life is that when I reach the end there will be a mass of people of all races and ethnicities, as far as the eye can see in all directions—children, adults, rich, poor, privileged, disadvantaged, powerful, oppressed, capable, disabled, in time and eternity—whose lives have been positively affected by Christ through me. I won't know them all because those directly touched by me multiplied exponentially.

Chapter 6

How Do I Relate to Others?

I don't know the key to success,
but the key to failure is trying to please everybody.
—Bill Cosby

We are all interconnected—friends, families, business organizations, and congregations. We influence these emotional systems and they naturally influence how we behave and relate. Every movement in the system affects every other individual part and the group as a whole.

To avoid regret in relating to others, give continual attention to your part in the system by gaining a clear definition of self and a clear understanding of the self-definitions of others and how we relate in a healthy, emotionally mature way.

Let's explore.

Definition of Self

Clarifying your relationships with others begins with increasing your clarity about who you are as an individual. This is called *differentiation of self*. We relate to others and they can relate to us on the basis of this understanding. The clearer your self-chosen definition, the more potential you have for mature relationships.

Living as a differentiated person requires that you make your own decisions about who you are in the context of family, friendships, organizations, and other emotional systems. In this process you create boundaries that define how you will be with others—what you will think and do—in the give-and-take relationships of the systems. The boundaries you create should reflect appropriate responsibility for self and others. As mature, self-differentiated individuals, we respect the boundaries of others as we hope they respect ours.

Making decisions related to differentiation of self requires that we be still, relax, think, and decide for ourselves. Times of high emotional anxiety, when we are tempted to either go with the crowd or walk away from the crowd and never come back, are the worst times for decisions about self-differentiation.

When we choose our own principles for living—what we will and won't do and what we will be and won't be—we tend to experience a happier, more satisfied life with healthier relationships, according to Ronald Richardson.[8] The balanced, self-differentiated person is a gift to those around them, helping everyone realize their potential.

You Will Be Pushed and Will Want to Push

As humans we are most comfortable with those whose thinking and behavior is familiar or like our own. When we decide about our self-definition and our boundaries, and live accordingly, we become relatively unfamiliar to others since we are decidedly different from them. They feel anxious; they resist our differences and push against our boundaries trying to get us to conform to their expectations. We might do the same to them. This can result in conflict.

The more clearly you define who you are and why you are here, the more you will notice differences between you and others. You might be aware that some people are easy to be with and some harder; that some people grind on your nerves and some people energize you.

As you grow in definition of self, you can more effectively:

- Cultivate the ability to interact with others in a way that is congenial and cooperative and allows other to do so, too.
- Surround yourself with people who nourish you and help you sense that you are valued, capable, loved, respected, and appreciated. Spend as little time as possible with those who discourage you or sap your energy.
- Cultivate the ability to nourish others. Generously help them sense that they are valued, capable, loved, respected, and appreciated.

In the process of nurturing and being nurtured, find in each relationship a balance between being too separate and too close. Find a balance between over-functioning and under-functioning in relationships. All of your relationships will not be perfectly balanced or enjoy the same degree of balance, but they can approximate healthy balance on a consistent basis.

What Are Separate and Close?

When you clarify your definition of self, you live in a more healthy way as an individual and in relation to others. You don't want to be so close to others that you lose your own identity. But you don't want to be so separate from others that you are cut off from them emotionally and relationally. Your best self and relationships to others are found in a balance between separate and close.

Close

Being connected is a good thing. By nature we are driven to seek love and approval through emotional connection with others. This same instinctive and automatic drive is present in everyone, and it pulls us together.

Our natural drive to connect and our need to manage anxiety by being close to others (as seen in animal herding), however, carry the danger of our becoming too close to others. We may try to be too much like others and think too much like them, creating a type of "group think." If we are too close, too interconnected—even to those we love most—we lose a part of ourselves and our identity to the other person and experience anxiety as a result. People who are this close tend to make decisions based more on their emotions than on their thinking. And as you know, this can lead to actions we regret.

Separate

Being an individual is a good thing. We are able to be healthier individuals through defining our selves. The push for such individuality rings in the phrases "Live out your uniqueness," "Be yourself, not somebody else," and "Live your own life."

Being too separate or disconnected, however, is not healthy. Through emotional isolation or geographic distance we can cut ourselves off from relationships and community. We can distance ourselves over time as a result of conflict, or as we assert our independence and isolate ourselves, separate, or withdraw from important relationships. This cut-off can increase anxiety. We need a balance between being connected in relationships and being appropriately self-defined and separate.

My client Frank told me that he doesn't like to hear people gossip or speak negatively of another person when that person is not present. So when he knows someone has a habit of doing this or suspects that they might speak ill of another, he avoids them altogether. He cuts himself off from them. Someone else might react differently and be drawn in, seeking approval, and talk about others when they aren't present or allow such talk in their presence.

In a recent coaching session I asked Frank what it would be like for him to stay connected with such a person but draw a boundary by saying something like "You know, I really appreciate our friendship and conversation but when I hear you speak badly of others I really feel uncomfortable. Could we talk about something else?" This step toward being close yet separate was a strong new awareness for Frank, and he began to spend more time with such people without betraying his own principles.

Balancing Function in Relationships

We can also benefit from finding a balance between over-functioning and under-functioning in relationships — a balance of give and take.

When a person over-functions, they are too dominant in the relationship. They know all, tell others how to think and what to do and feel, help too much, are overly responsible for others, do things for others that they can do for themselves, and demand agreement. They might believe others are the problem and they are or have the solution. Those who consistently over-function can do very well in life, but they can be miserable in the process and make those around them miserable as well.

When someone under-functions, they are passive and take all that the over-functioners have to give. They can be overly dependent on others; let others tell them what to think, do, and feel; seek advice or help when it's really not needed; ask others to do for them what they can do for themselves; embrace the thinking of the group without evaluation; and give in at every nudge. They can come to believe that they are the problem. A person who consistently under-functions can become physically, mentally, emotionally, or socially ill.

We can alternate between the two extremes. Most do. It's best to find a balance that embodies healthy give and take. We can assess our relative over- and under-functioning through reflection, communication with others, and enlisting the help of professionals. Sometimes an outside viewpoint is most helpful.

Anxiety

Some describe anxiety as any strong negative emotion. It is contagious in the emotional system of relationships. Individuals pass it along like a virus. Anxiety goes wherever the system allows it to.

Anxiety is an automatic emotional response of which we are mostly unaware. It can be a sense of being uptight, tense, protective, and even panicky, and is sometimes described as the fight, flight, or freeze reaction. Anxiety itself is not a problem, and can be helpful; it is a natural part of living. But because our relational systems are by nature emotional (anxious), emotions strongly influence how we relate in these systems.

The basic source of anxiety is our lower brain which is like a reptile's brain—reactive rather than thinking and rational.

The intensity of our anxiety is relative. We can experience acute spikes in anxiety in reaction to life events such as a car accident, injury, crisis, or conflict. We also carry a level of anxiety (also known as *chronic anxiety*) with us on a daily basis.

Think about a time when someone confronted you and reprimanded you or told you off. When this happened, your reactive, reptilian brain kicked into gear and your anxiety increased. You had no time to think, but rather reacted, ducked, swerved, ran, or defended yourself. Physical symptoms arose with the anxiety; you experienced an adrenalin rush and probably felt your face flush.

When you're highly anxious, the reactive, reptilian part of the brain is highly active. At the same time, your thinking, rational brain is less active, rational thinking slows, your perspective narrows dramatically, and creative thought is lost. When anxious, your imagination freezes, curiosity is disabled, options are seen as limited (black and white), questions are replaced by declarations, positions are taken while your principles in regard to them become blurry, and quick fixes become the primary consideration. **An anxious person can become defensive on multiple levels and even have feelings of helplessness.**

When negative emotions or anxiety arise in you, you might want to act on them to address the threat without thinking through the consequences. But emotions are primarily signals, and not a good basis on which to make decisions. Irrational, reactive behavior is negative and undesirable to others, and can damage relationships.

Managing Anxiety in Relationships

When a friend or family member has had a bad day, they might bring anxiety (strong emotions) to the time you spend together. It's only natural that you then get caught up in their anxiety or upset with them. Before long both of you are anxious, and then—what do you know—the person who brought their anxiety to the table feels better and you feel worse. If someone else then joins the two of you, you can pass the anxiety on to them and the two of you feel better while the third person feels worse. You've probably noticed this in your relationships.

You can decide whether or not you will "channel" the anxiety of another person or be anxious about a threat to you, real or perceived. You can keep a lid on your anxiety and hold it inside up to a point, but it is still uncomfortable and is apparent in the way you "show up" with others.

Be a Calm, Rational Presence

You have a choice about whether or not to become anxious or caught up in the anxiety of another person. Being calm, and engaging yourself and others in rational thought, makes systems healthier and more productive.

The key is planning. **Decide ahead of time what you will do in the face of anxiety, and let what would have been your reaction become a calm, rational response.** Here are some tips to help you be ready:
1. In quiet moments of thought:
   a. Accept that you will face anxiety several times daily.

    b. Draw boundaries to identify what you will and won't allow from others, and what you will and won't do when anxiety arises.

    c. Determine what you will do to move from reaction to appropriate response.

    d. Practice your chosen response over and over at different times.

2. When anxiety presents itself:

    a. Let your initial response be to take several deep belly breaths and relax your shoulders and hands. This is your body telling your emotions what to do: Relax.

    b. Time-outs are always good. Excuse yourself to the restroom, relax, and think.

    c. Use assertiveness techniques.

    d. Ask questions. The quickest way I know to engage rational thought is to ask questions. Ask questions of yourself, others, and of your own emotions.

Questions for yourself about the situation:
- What do I really want of this?
- What do I believe about it?
- What are my unfounded assumptions?
- What do I fear in this?
- What is most valuable to me in this?
- Why do I care about this?

Questions for yourself about your emotions:
- What is this emotion? *Ask this to clarify what you are actually feeling. Sometimes you simply need to acknowledge the emotion, name it, and go on to something else.*
- What does this emotion signal? What does it mean?

Questions for others:
- How did you come to this thinking?
- What do you hope will come out of this?
- What is most important to you in this?
- What perspective do you have about this?
- What common interests do we have about this?

When asking yourself questions, write your answers down whenever possible. When you ask questions of others, listen attentively and ask follow-up questions with curiosity. This helps get everyone into a less emotional, more rational frame of mind in which issues become clearer and you can make progress toward a common goal.

My client Mary's boss was described by a psychologist as a dry alcoholic—abusive, then apologetic, promising never to do it again, then abusive, apologetic again, etc.

One night he "chewed her out" in a public place. Mary determined that he would not do this to her again. Sometime later he called her to his office with an unstated agenda. He began raging and ranting and shaking his finger in her face.

Acting on the plans she'd made in a time of quiet, calm thought for dealing with her anxiety, she quietly and gently closed her portfolio, stood up, and began to walk to the door. With her hand on the doorknob, she calmly said, "It might be good if we continue this at a time when you are feeling better."

Still shouting, he asked her what her problem was. She told him that she did not want to be spoken to in that manner. After a few minutes he was able to calm down, she went back and sat down, and they were able to complete the meeting.

Mary had no intention of channeling his anxiety or being over-controlled by him. She drew the boundaries and stood by them. She had determined to be the non-anxious, rational presence in the room, protecting the boundaries she had set previously. She was determined not to do or say anything she'd later regret.

It's a Choice

Choosing is a function of rational thought. *Self-chosen* means that you thought through and chose for yourself versus someone else doing your thinking and choosing for you.

Choice is an action we take after we think through to conclusions. Some choices are impulsive or reactive, which means they had little thought behind them. Some are emotional and might have no thought behind them. These are reactions, not decisions.

Avoiding regret involves deciding in advance how you will relate to others. By gaining a clear definition of *self* and living in balance, you can go through your life with the rewarding sense that you have given and received and have not compromised the unique person and mission that is you.

Faith Sticky Note: **Love Is the Rule**

My relationships with others are guided by the law of love. The greatest commandment as defined by Jesus involves loving God, loving others, and loving self.

The word for this love in the original language of the New Testament is *agape*. In classical Greek this word primarily referred to honor given to another person. A brief but profound summary of Jesus Christ's actions—not emotions—in Phil. 2:5-11 illustrates the redefinition of love.

- Love is not impulse of feelings or necessarily a natural inclination.
- Love is not motivated by whether or not the object deserves it.
- Love seeks the opportunity to do good to all.
- Love is a deliberate choice, which may be expressed in maximum measure through sacrifice.

PERFORM: Taking Action to Avoid Regret

Here is your call to courageous, responsible action. So far you have planned. Now it's time to act.

I once heard a therapist whom I highly respect say, "The lives of people are characterized by two great master stories. One is 'I am a victim.' The other is "I am responsible."

You can allow the master story of your life to be that of the victim, trying to account for every life experience as something having been done to you by other people or circumstances. This takes living out of your control.

Or you can be the courageous, responsible person who takes action to own your situation and makes progress to be more, see more, and achieve more. Even those who have been unjustly victimized can be courageous and responsible in dealing with their victimization.

Chapter 7

Live According to Your Boundaries

Good fences make good neighbors.

—Robert Frost

Fences are good things. They are boundaries that define and contain. Fences have gates that allow movement out and in. It's important to have good fences—good boundaries—in order to take action toward a life without regret.

You Know You Have Boundary Problems When...

You are Overly Concerned about Pleasing

You might find yourself going along with others, bending over backward to please them, or allowing yourself to be a doormat for fear they will be displeased with you or reject you.

Many years ago the Abilene Paradox was made popular by Jerry Harvey. The Abilene Paradox involves the story of a family playing dominoes on the porch in the hot summer in Coleman, Texas. Someone suggested they go to Abilene for dinner, which involved a lengthy, somewhat uncomfortable trip. No one really wanted to go, but no one spoke up, so they went on what became a miserable trip to Abilene.

The Abilene Paradox is a type of boundary failure. It is the curious proclivity of people to go along with group ideas or decisions with which they totally disagree. As a result, the group takes action that contradicts what the members silently agree they really want, but they don't speak up with their opinions. This is a type of group-think in which individuals do not courageously stand up for what they believe is best. They fear rejection. They want to please others and avoid risk. They withhold their opinions because they imagine all kinds of negative outcomes and would rather go along to get along. You need not "go to Abilene" if you don't want to go. Speak up with your opinion and establish your boundaries. Be responsible.

When You Take Too Much Responsibility for Others

Another indicator of inappropriate boundaries is taking too much responsibility for the lives of others—you try to tell others what to think, how to think, and how to feel. You might try to help too much, doing things for others that they can do for themselves, or even try to force agreement.

You might also take responsibility for others' emotions about your boundaries. Keep in mind that you cannot control others' emotions. You do not make another person mad, sad, or glad; they choose it. They are responsible for their own emotions, including those they may have about your boundaries.

I have heard so many people say, "I would take such-and-such action, but I don't want to hurt their feelings." If you assume this posture, you will take very little action in your life, because emotions are easily affected. And people tend to hang on to that emotional pain. They choose whether or not to hold on to the hurt. Some of us choose to be mad, sad, or glad quicker and for a longer period than others.

Creating Boundaries Is Hard Work

My grandfather was a farmer. I was privileged to spend several weeks with him and Grandma during the summers for several years during my childhood and adolescence. Occasionally Granddad determined that a new fence was needed. He did what he called "studying about it," which meant he was thinking it through. He decided where it would be and marked the place.

Some of the hardest work we did was building fences. We dug the holes with post-hole diggers. This was a blood, sweat, and tears kind of hand tool. You lift the tool up, drive it into the ground, pull out some dirt, and repeat until you have a deep hole into which you can put the fence post. When done with one post, you repeat the process until all the posts are in. Then you stretch the wire from post to post, using a hammer and large staples to attach the wire to the posts. Repeat the process until done. All under the Texas summer sun.

Creating personal boundaries is hard work, too. Identifying the locations of the boundaries you want to build is part of the work you have been doing so far in your definition of self. You are in the process of defining who you are and who you are not, what you will do and what you won't do, how you will be with others and how you will not be, and how you will allow them to be with you and what you will not allow. Creating a boundary can be as simple as asking and then expecting someone to knock before entering your room, or as complex as determining how responsible you will be for the feelings and needs of others.

Once in a while Granddad's cattle would be found outside the fence, which was a signal that someone left a gate open or the fence was down somewhere. Little time was lost to close the gate or mend the fence and get the cattle back inside since they were usually grazing in a money crop, which, obviously, was a costly problem. Or they could be munching delightedly in a neighbor's garden. Worse, they could be on the road and in danger of being hit by a vehicle, which could injure or kill both the cow and the occupants of the vehicle. Granddad's fences protected lives, livelihoods, relationships, and the cattle themselves.

Your boundaries protect you and others. They allow you to live appropriately separate, yet close to others. Once you have defined some boundaries, it is important to keep them clearly in view and well maintained. Sometimes repairs are needed, and the need for repairs reminds you and others what is to be inside and what is to be outside.

Gates Give Controlled Options

All Granddad's fences had at least one gate and sometimes more. From time to time we'd move the cattle, which required opening the gates and moving the cattle out of one pasture and guiding them to another fenced pasture. The gates also allowed us a level of convenience and freedom of movement without having to climb the fence or take it down.

Boundaries need controlled permeability. They need the flexibility of a gate or two. Without this flexibility, boundaries can shut people out. If too flexible, they allow others too much freedom and allow us to take too much freedom with the boundaries of others.

You can control these "gates" by opening them briefly if something needs to be allowed in or out. For example, you can open a gate to let activities that don't exactly fit your purpose in and out on appropriate occasions. You decide appropriateness. Another example is opening a gate to allow someone to emotionally vent in hopes that this clearing will open the way for responsible, rational, and productive behavior.

Be careful not to open a gate too often, too widely, or for too long, or to leave it unattended. There is danger in leaving a gate flapping open and, as a result, having no real boundary at all. Keep the gate closed until you see the need to open it.

Define Your Boundaries

While you work on defining your boundaries, what you want to be inside them will become much clearer. These bounded areas might be related to items previously treated in this book, and more, such as:

- What is uniquely you (self)
- What is important to you (values)
- Why you believe you are here (purpose)
- Actions you will take (behaviors)
- What you are responsible for
- Where you will go
- Things and people that help and nurture you
- Feelings you will keep
- Beliefs and convictions that are yours
- Attitudes you will nurture in yourself
- What is true for you
- What thoughts you will allow yourself to have
- How and what you will allow others to speak to you
- How you will allow others to act toward you

Just as certain things will be inside your boundaries, there are also things that will be outside your boundaries. These are things that are not you, you will not allow, you will not say, you will not do, and so forth.

For example, if you are pressured to act contrary to your fundamental personality, that likely falls outside your boundary and is something you should not do. Maybe you prefer to be with only a few people, and others pressure you to be with bigger groups than you prefer. Be a person of integrity, consistent on the outside with who you are on the inside.

If an activity doesn't fit within the purpose you've determined for your

life (the boundary), the general rule is: Don't do it. Life is too short to spend time on something that is not a part of your calling and purpose.

If you are pressured to act contrary to your values, *don't do it*. Doing so would be the easy way out, and you'll very likely experience feelings of regret afterward.

Communicate Your Boundaries

Once you have determined your boundaries, don't expect people to guess or intuit what those boundaries are. Take action to make them clear for others by kindly, graciously, honestly, clearly, and firmly communicating your boundaries to them. Boundaries are your "yes" and "no" for relating to yourself and the world.

Boundaries can be communicated in a variety of ways. At Granddad's, the barbed wire fence was visible. If livestock got too close they could feel the barbs. In some instances, Granddad used wire that would give a mild though attention-getting shock when touched. When the livestock touched the electric fence, they bucked and kicked and were off to another part of the pasture away from the fence.

TAKE ACTION: You don't need an electric fence to communicate your boundaries. You need clear, sometimes very firm verbal communication to let others know where you stand, what is allowed, and what is not. Calm, rational conversations are excellent ways to clarify your boundaries for others and to understand their boundaries.

Expect Pressure on Your Boundaries

Granddad's livestock couldn't care less about the fences until the fences prevented them from having something they wanted. The livestock would occasionally push the fences. Sometimes they just want to be "out." If they could get out of a weakened fence they would. If they could get through a fence designed to keep them out, they would.

Just because you tell others where your boundaries are, doesn't mean everyone will be happy or celebrate this with you. It's human nature to be uncomfortable at some level with the boundaries of others; your friends and loved ones will be uncomfortable with yours and you with theirs, even if the discomfort is only very slight.

When your boundaries are in place and visible, you can expect pushback and even sabotage from others, as the boundaries may restrict how they act around you and interact with you. Remember, people want you to be and act according to their expectations. It's like a border dispute of sorts.

For example, if someone speaks to you in a disrespectful way, you can communicate a boundary, using the assertiveness techniques I outline in the next chapter, by saying, "When you speak to me in that way, I feel disrespected. Please don't speak to me that way again."

Some individuals have no boundaries and respect none. They are self-focused, have difficulty regulating their behavior and telling themselves "No." They disrespectfully run roughshod over everyone and everything. You can allow this or you can stop it at your boundary. These individuals often do not learn from experience so you will need to remind them of your boundaries more than once.

Those who are more self-aware, socially aware, and emotionally mature, and have a clearer definition of self and clearer boundaries for themselves, will more likely appreciate your definition and boundaries, as well as your courage in placing them. They will more readily respect and honor your boundaries. Keep in mind that they won't be perfect along these lines and you won't either.

When others push your boundaries, you have several choices: Hold the boundary, compromise on your boundary (move it), open the gate on the boundary, or remove it altogether. Others have the same choices when we press against their boundaries.

Remember that you can do some boundary pushing of your own. But it's important for you to honor the boundaries of others just as you expect them to honor yours. This means you give up trying to control, manipulate, or force them to adjust their boundaries to suit you. Respect their boundaries and live with them in a way that is balanced between separate and close and between over- and under-functioning.

Plan to Hold Your Boundaries

Holding our boundaries consistently is a challenge because we naturally want people to like us and approve of us. In setting boundaries, we fear rejection, hurting others, anger from others, shame, and being seen as selfish. Some even believe that standing up for themselves is a violation of religious or spiritual principles.

Plan ahead for how you will communicate and protect your boundaries when they are threatened. Planning for this in a calm, quiet time, away from the heat of the moment, prepares you for a much more rational response in the face of a threat to your boundaries. When you need to communicate or protect a boundary, use the assertiveness techniques in the next chapter and be firm. You need not be angry or overbearing, but don't be a wimp either.

The support team I describe in Chapter 14 can assist you in creating boundaries and keeping them in place, and support you when things get difficult. Even though a life with good boundaries can seem lonely, it is empowered and full of integrity.

Boundaries Help Everyone

You might see the setting of boundaries as helping only you. Actually your clear boundaries help others know how to be with you and what to expect when they are with you. Children are healthier both emotionally and socially when they are reared with clear boundaries and are fully responsible for clearly defined consequences when they violate boundaries. In relationships, not much is different—boundaries, responsibility, consequences. You won't likely send your adult friends for a "time out," but you can provide a mature, firm reminder when they violate a boundary. In extreme cases you might want to withdraw from the relationship until such time as your boundary is fully respected.

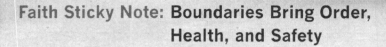

Faith Sticky Note: Boundaries Bring Order, Health, and Safety

Some look at all of the legal boundaries of the Old Testament and believe they portray God as a cosmic kill-joy whose purpose is to make people miserable. Jesus summed up these boundaries as loving God, loving others, and loving self. Is it possible that God conferred these mandates to lovingly protect His people, preserve society and community, and keep them closely related to Him—He who cared most for them and His creation?

Peter adjusted a boundary with Jesus. He impulsively set a boundary denying Jesus the opportunity to wash his feet at the Last Supper. Jesus explained the importance of His actions to Peter, and Peter chose to adjust his boundary. In fact he did away with it altogether, allowing Jesus to wash his feet and even his whole body. Like Peter, we must choose boundaries reasonably and then adjust them as needed.

Chapter 8

Live According to Your Plan: Assertiveness

It's easier to act your way into a new way of feeling
than to feel your way into a new way of acting.

—Gordon Allport

Once you have created boundaries through defining your self, vocation, values, mission, and vision, an essential tool you can use for managing boundaries and living without regret is assertiveness.

Individuals use a range of personal styles to protect boundaries and relate to others: passive, aggressive, passive-aggressive, and assertive.

Passive

When you employ a passive style, you appear reserved and too easygoing, giving others permission to walk over your wishes, needs, interests, emotions, beliefs, and opinions. You fail to stand up for yourself, or stand up for yourself in such an ineffective way that you allow your rights to be easily violated. You might be overly apologetic or tentative and ambiguous. You might also employ a victim mentality and use guilt to manipulate others.

Aggressive

Aggressive behavior is that of a bully who humiliates, intimidates, and walks over the wishes, needs, interests, feelings, beliefs, and opinions of others. If you're too aggressive, you stand up for yourself in a way that violates the rights of others. You might humiliate, control, punish, or put down others in order to enforce your own rights. An aggressive person often exaggerates, over-generalizes, threatens, labels, and blames others to protect themselves.

Passive-Aggressive

If you're passive-aggressive, you move in subtle, indirect ways to express aggression, anger, or frustration. You appear passive, but in reality you make subversive efforts to sabotage others. This conduct can manifest as intentional undermining, sulking, procrastinating, sarcasm, backstabbing, playing the victim, distrust, resistance, or covert hostility. You want others to feel guilty and manipulate them with guilt, but you won't tell others what is bothering you. Instead you slam doors and drawers, drop hints, and use the silent treatment.

Assertive

If you are assertive, you hold your boundaries for your own wishes, needs, interests, feelings, beliefs, and opinions while respecting those of others. You stand up for yourself in a way that does not violate the basic rights of others. **The good news is that anyone can learn to use this style.**

Being assertive involves direct, clear, tactfully honest, and appropriate expression of your emotions and thoughts. This kind of communication is considerate of the other person's wishes, needs, interests, feelings, beliefs, and opinions. If you're assertive, you're responsibly confrontational in expressing positive and corrective suggestions to others. Unlike the passive or passive-aggressive person, you state your true thoughts and emotions, directly request what you want, and tactfully refuse unreasonable requests.

Being assertive does not mean that you can say whatever is on your mind no matter what. It does not mean that you are guaranteed to get your way. It does not mean that you can unload on someone. When someone pushes or crosses your boundaries, counting to ten or taking a time-out to cool down are good tools to use, even before an assertive response.

I encourage you to be assertive more often and consistently. In the 1950s, behaviorist Joseph Wolpe discovered that nearly everyone can be assertive in some situations and not at all in others. His research also showed that assertiveness and anxiety cannot coexist.[9] If you practice assertiveness in your interactions, you might feel less depressed, angry, resentful, and anxious in relationships.

TAKE ACTION: Good Communication

Good communication in general can help you preserve your boundaries and keep you from doing or saying things that you later regret. Keep your statements and questions short, simple, and specific. As a coach I describe this as being "laser-like" in your communication. Listen deeply to the speaker, paying attention to body language, facial expressions, and the tone, pace, and pitch of their voice. In an effort to clarify and fully understand, paraphrase back to the speaker what you believe they said. Ask them what they understood you to say. To encourage dialogue, ask honest, open-ended questions that allow for more than yes, no, or limited answers.

Assertive communication is strengthened by relaxed, confident body language. Look the other person in the eye, but don't stare them down. Use a calm voice tone with a natural pitch and an even pace. Support your voice with plenty of air, but don't whisper.

"I" messages are crucial to assertive communication. The use of "I" allows you to speak for yourself in a non-accusatory fashion. Avoid the use of "you" or "we." This keeps the receiver of your assertive communication off the defensive, and the anxiety—yours included—at a lower level.

Do not use email, texting, notes, or letters for communication that carries an emotional load. When you do, there is a high risk of miscommunication, because you lose 93 percent of your communicative ability due to the missing body language, facial expressions, and voice qualities. Make an appointment to meet with the person face to face. When this is impossible, a phone call works, but is a distant second to meeting in person.

Loving Assertion

Acting with love toward others and yourself often means standing your ground and compassionately asserting your boundaries. You can be sure that this will create discomfort and anxiety for those who encounter your boundaries. As you hold the line, those affected might say, "You don't love me."

Some have described *loving assertion* as a type of "tough love." Employing tough love entails defining your relationships with others and acting assertively and resolutely on your definition.

Lauren, my daughter, sometimes reminded me, "Dad, you told us we could disagree if we did it respectfully, and I think…" She and our son-in-law are both public elementary school teachers. I am so pleased that they use loving assertion with the children in their classes to discipline without damaging. They are very adept at using these same skills with one another and in their broader relationships.

If someone behaves badly toward you, chances are good that they are doing the same to others and sabotaging their relationships. Those who do not respect others' boundaries are often intimidating and, as a result, often receive very little honest feedback and challenges regarding their behavior. If you assertively hold your boundaries against undesirable behavior toward you, providing feedback as allowed, you and the individual who is behaving badly can benefit in ways far beyond your immediate relationship. Loving assertion can help them learn to respect others more and to respect themselves as well.

Some Assertiveness Basics

The following are a few common assertiveness techniques to get you started. Take care to use the general recommendations above.

Broken Record

Use the broken record when someone seems unrelenting and determined to pressure you into doing what they want you to do. For example, let's say a coworker is trying to get you to stay late at work to help them get a project done—"pleeease"—which will make you late for a family dinner.

There is no need to use a nuclear device when a small rock will do. Start with the minimal response, such as "I'm sorry, I won't be able to help you this time." If they ask again, repeat exactly the same statement without embellishment or elaboration. If they don't get it, escalate your response, saying, "No, I will not be able to help you." If they still don't get it, firmly and kindly call a halt to the conversation by saying, "The answer is no. Please don't ask again."

You can also use the broken record when the person's behavior toward you is offensive. I've used this a time or two with raging supervisors. In a calm, firm voice, I say, "I do not want you to shout at me. Please stop." I continue to mark the boundary by repeating exactly the same statement without embellishment or elaboration. If the person can come back to a rational position, they will calm down and be able to continue a reasonably productive conversation. Otherwise you might need to escalate by firmly, calmly telling them to "Stop now or we will need to reschedule this meeting."

You may be thinking, "Saying something like that could cost me my job." That's always possible. But do you really want to work for someone who is constantly pushing or raging? Life is too short for that. Have courage.

Notice that the broken record is not an attack. It is taking a stand for your values and boundaries. If you use this technique, people will eventually get the idea that you have a boundary that you won't allow them to push through.

Fogging

Another technique is fogging. When someone tries to push their position or get you to do things their way, simply acknowledge their position without agreeing or disagreeing, using a simple statement such as "I understand that _____ works for you and I feel just fine doing it my way." Do not argue or depict you as right and them as wrong. Just use a statement like the one above. Couple this with the broken record if needed.

Apology

There will likely be times when you receive criticism and you must simply acknowledge it as bona fide by offering an apology. Here is a technique for offering an apology that has excellent potential for achieving an emotionally healthy closure: When apologizing, don't look out of the corners of your eyes and say, "Sorry." Don't say, "Well, if I did, I'm sorry." When it comes to an apology, use no ifs, ands, or buts. Keep it short, simple, and focused on the issue, saying, "I apologize for _____. Will you forgive me?" Wait for a response.

The question allows for closure of the incident or issue regardless of their response. If they accept your apology, thank them. If you sincerely offered the apology and request, and they don't accept, you have done all you can. Let it go.

Negative Assertion

We all make errors. We all have faults. We all have weaknesses. Some make it their mission to fix you. If they believe you are not hearing them, they will work even harder to do so. Use negative assertion by accepting your errors and faults (without apology). Agree with the criticism, strongly and sympathetically. Even if the person is nitpicking, negative assertion can help get them off your back so you can take the time you need to decide whether the error, fault, or weakness is something that needs your attention. You can simply say something like "You know, I could have done that differently" or "I could improve on that."

Free Conversation

Free conversation is a great assertiveness technique. I've used it more times than I can tell. When confronted by an angry individual, mentally frame the situation as a *conversation* versus a *confrontation*. Your natural inclination is to hurry up and get out of there or to set them straight right then and there. Instead, ask open-ended questions that call for more than a yes, no, or otherwise limited answer. Make requests for more information such as "Help me understand more about _____," "Say more about _____," or "Tell me more about _____." Ask with a genuine interest in understanding and listen to their response.

Feedback

When a person's behavior is rude, mean, unkind, hurtful, inconsiderate, or disrespectful, you can draw a boundary to state what is out of bounds and what is in bounds. Start by objectively describing the offending behavior. Express your thoughts or feelings using "I" messages. Inquire about the intent behind the person's behavior. Specify what you want or what you would prefer using "I" messages. Describe the positive results that can come from an agreement about the boundaries.

For example, let's say that in a team meeting Joe consistently interrupts you and tries to complete your sentences or thoughts. Outside the meeting you might say to him, "Joe, when you interrupt me and try to complete my thoughts in team meetings, I feel disrespected and demeaned, and it throws my train of thought off track. Is that your intent?"

Wait for a yes or no response. After the response state, "I would prefer it if I could complete my own thoughts and sentences and not be interrupted when I speak in team meetings. If I am able to do this, I believe I can make a stronger contribution to the issues at hand and I will be able to hear you more effectively. How would you be willing to work with me on this?"

Don't Take Responsibility for Their Response

As you practice assertiveness, remember that you do not make another person mad, sad, glad, or have any other emotion. Nor do they make you feel emotions. We choose our emotions. When an emotion arises, the individual is responsible for what they do with it. They can put it away or nurture it.

Others are not responsible for your emotions either.

Deliver your assertive message and do not take responsibility for how others feel about it. You do not hurt their feelings; they choose to be hurt.

Faith Sticky Note: **Too Nice**

Some common false beliefs in Christian circles, and those of other religions as well, is that to assertively hold boundaries is to be unkind, selfish, and not Christ-like. Such thinking can create a nasty relational mess in congregations and groups in which these beliefs are held. The mess created weakens the ability of the congregation to communicate God's message and robs the congregation of its credibility, casting a shadow on its ministry.

Assertively held boundaries can bring order and health to relationships and strength to a congregation. Jesus Christ had boundaries. We need go no further than His temptation in the wilderness just prior to the inauguration of His ministry to see those boundaries. While saying no to some things, He was saying yes to others. He was assertive with the religious leaders of the day and with His disciples.

Paul and other positive individuals in Scripture seem to have clearly differentiated self and associated boundaries. Their words and actions protected their values, purpose, vision, and calling even though others tried to influence them otherwise. As needed, they strongly asserted themselves to ensure their faithfulness to who they were and where they were going.

Chapter 9

Managing Your Priorities

The feeling of being hurried is not usually the result of living a full life and having no time. It is, on the contrary born of a vague fear that we are wasting our life. When we do not do the one thing we ought to do, we have not time for anything else —we are the busiest people in the world.

—Eric Hoffer

There was once a time when people sat on a porch or in a parlor to visit, read, write, play an instrument, or sing. I recall long periods of sitting, visiting, playing, and enjoying one another when I visited my grandparents on their farm. When it was time to work, it was time to work, and that was the priority. When it was time to play, fish, or just visit, it was time to do that. That was the priority. Because mobility was limited, people could not just run here and there. I don't recall any references to hurrying or the need to rush. Those words were not in our vocabulary, and we had very enjoyable, productive times together.

How Are You?

"I am so busy." You've heard it and you've said it. And these days, people don't say it. They just drop their shoulders, roll their eyes, and sigh. Some seem to believe that being busy justifies their existence, and wear it as a badge.

Today a slow lifestyle is uncomfortable for many us of. We are more mobile and have more information, more opportunities, and more demands on us than ever. There seems to be a drive to hurry here and there, always busy going and doing.

When we force too much busy-ness into the time we have, we feel hurried, frustrated, discouraged, and sometimes out of control without a clear sense of purpose, focus, and accomplishment. Some say we have the "hurry sickness," which leads to stress and poor emotional, physical, and relational health. We end up regretting time that is wasted, opportunities we miss because we're busy, and time not spent on what matters.

What's it like for you and your family, friends, and business colleagues?

Time Management?

Time is uncontrollable. It moves on even when we don't do anything in it. Time is a truly nonrenewable resource. We all have a fixed amount of time in the cycle of seasons and of nights and days.

People say they need help with their *time management*. I firmly believe this term is a misnomer. **If we are to live without regret, we must see our task as managing what we do *in* time instead of what we do *with* time. We don't manage time; we manage what we *do* in time.**

Goals

Goals that keep you from regret are consistent with your definition of self and values, and lead to the fulfillment of your vocation, mission, and vision. They help you decide what to do in time. The most powerful progress is founded on goals that are clear and measurable. The acronym SMART has been used to define the qualities needed in goals:

Specific (lose ten pounds versus get healthier)
Measurable (use a yardstick to show how much, how many, etc.)
Achievable (they are realistic, yet challenging)
Relevant (they align with your values, purpose, and vision)
Time-bound (they have a deadline)

Reassess your goals often enough to keep them aligned and help you maintain forward progress.

Use goals, as any other tool, to serve you instead of you serving them. If a tool becomes too complicated or high-maintenance, you have created a monster that wastes your time and is counterproductive; the tool becomes your priority (and a distraction) instead of serving the purpose for which it's intended.

Priorities: How Do You Decide?

By definition, a priority is what comes ahead of something else. When applied to a group of tasks or responsibilities, it is something that is given first position and other things are positioned in descending order of importance. If you enforce the priority, you keep "first things first" and protect yourself from a chaotic, frenzied existence.

By determining your definition of self, values, vocation, mission, and vision you have made big decisions about what you will do in the time you have. When you set related goals, these create even greater clarity and focus. As you tightly focus your activities on your goals, these activities become your priorities. Hopefully you will create some boundaries and limitations that will help protect your priorities.

Personally, I have determined to stop doing more and resolved to do more that really matters. I frequently use these questions to help narrow my focus to what really matters and simplify my life:

- What is the most important thing I can do in the time I have?
- What can I do that will yield value that money cannot buy and death cannot take away?
- What can I do that will live beyond my death?

What is most important to you? What has priority? Toward what are you working? What you do in time tells the tale. I wonder what your time use says about your goals and priorities now.

You can complete a time study to see what you are really doing with the time you have. For a Time Log Template that will help with a revealing study of your time use, go to www.DiscoverYourTrueCourse.com/reader-bonus and download your free copy.

You can allow people and things to take your focus off your priorities, decrease your progress toward goals, waste your energy, and create lots of opportunities for regret down the road. Below are a few tips to help you avoid this and stay focused on what matters.

In the not-too-distant past, you had to wait to get to a phone and wait for the mailman to come. This waiting time was time for rest. But now communication occurs in seconds through a constant onslaught of cell phone calls, email, and text messages from anywhere on the globe. The speed of communication creates pressure and stress that can drain you, violate your boundaries, and demand time away from your purpose... if you let it. People use these modes of communication to try to push you to serve their priorities, accomplish their interests, keep their schedule, and respond to their requests immediately. Remember, very little requires an instantaneous response. Don't get caught in this trap.

Think First

Before initiating any type of communication—phone, email, text, or others—ask some important questions to help determine what is best:
- Is this really necessary?
- Will it save time and effort for those involved?
- Is it the best communication method for this instance?

When you make business calls or expect to receive business calls, be prepared for the conversation. List items to be covered and gather all needed information prior to making or receiving the call. While on the call, be specific and concise. Of course, if the call is just a friendly visit, none of the above applies. Enjoy it.

Control the Communication

- Make phone appointments to save enormous amounts of time playing phone tag.
- Batch. Set blocks of time to make calls, receive calls, send texts and emails, and respond to texts and email. Instant responses to individual texts and emails waste time.
- Set your email software to manual send/receive, and send/receive mail just twice daily.
- Turn off all automatic notifications on your computer and phone; they create distractions that cost about twenty-five minutes of productive time for each notification.
- Use caller ID, your assistant, or assigned ring tones, or allow your phone to go to voicemail and screen the voicemails. Give your assistant a list of those with whom you must speak.
- Value the people present over people calling. If one of your top values is family, and they are included in your purpose statement, please put your phone away when you are with them. I often watch moms

and dads in stores and restaurants who ignore their kids for the sake of their phones, texts, emails, and social media on their phones. They seem to be unable to put them down. What does it say to your children, spouse, family, and friends when they are talking with you and you take your phone out to give it the attention that *they* deserve? How much initiation of important dialogue with your spouse or children is lost because the phone is the default for you attention?

- Furnish your own phone to avoid being a slave to your work phone. If you must use only the company phone, treat the calls and other communications as described above and take time out from it regularly for your own self-care.
- Use a scheduler like TimeTrade.com to allow people to schedule meetings and appointments with you rather than using ten email exchanges to choose a time and place.
- Don't allow internet notifications to be pushed to your phone. Set aside a time to start checking all those interesting bits of information on your own without the push, and be sure to set a stop time. Set a timer if needed.
- For social networking and internet surfing, note the time you start and set a time to end. Use a timer if needed. Ask yourself, "How is this contributing to my goals and in alignment with my priorities?"

Staying Focused — Managing People

Drop-in visitors can create another type of costly distraction. I just got out of a session with a client whose employee can't say no to drop-ins. As a result the employee spends most of the day visiting with drop-ins and answering their needs to the detriment of his projects. He is social enough to enjoy it as well. But his productivity is lower than desired.

At work, customarily treat drop-ins as "howdy" visits. You can send messages to this effect as you come out of your office to greet them. Do not sit down. Stand. Get to the point by offering a friendly greeting and ask, "How can I help you today?" If the drop-in has a real need, it is likely it will require more than a few minutes, so try to schedule an appointment time or another time to visit. This can help you and the drop-in to be more efficient and productive.

Staying Focused—Productivity Practices

You can adopt personal qualities and take actions that will help you focus on your priorities so you don't later regret lost opportunity. Make conscious efforts to deal more effectively with personal issues and practices that delay, hinder, and hold you back from those priorities.

- **Don't multi-task.** Recent brain science demonstrates that we are not at all effective when we try to multi-task. Our brains focus on only one task at a time. Trying to do more than one thing at a time increases errors, lowers quality of output, and increases stress levels.
- **Layer activities.** While one task is completing without your attention, you can attend to another. An example of layering is allowing a program to download to your computer while you work on something else or allowing one dish to cook while you prepare another. Layering can increase productivity.
- **Batch tasks.** Grouping similar tasks together can make what you do in time more efficient. If you need to run errands, plan all your errands to be included in one trip. If you have phone calls to make, group them together.
- **Use wait-time.** While waiting anywhere, use your smart phone, laptop, tablet computer, or notepad to work toward your goals. Keep reading or writing material with you at all times. Meditate, use stress-relief strategies, or do memory work.
- **Avoid mind clutter.** Whether you use a high-tech device or pencil and scratch pad, write down whatever it is you need to remember. Use a calendar and a task list, and create notifications on your electronic device to remind you. Treat your smart phone as a productivity tool rather than simply a phone or a game source.
- **Avoid procrastination.** There are many reasons for it, but don't spend time figuring out why you procrastinate. Whatever you need to do, simply do it now.
- **Communicate clearly.** Check for understanding on the part of the receiver of your communication. Don't assume the receiver understood anything you said.
- **Be decisive.** Develop the habit of good decision-making by doing what is necessary to gather the information, reduce the issue to its simplest terms, and make a decision.

Making Room for Your Priorities

Each of your activities takes up room in your schedule, your mental capacity, and your energy. Simply establishing priorities establishes to what you will give room. Here are actions you can take and skills you can develop to make more room for your priorities:

- Work in your areas of strength.
- Delegate your areas of weakness to the strengths of others. There are a variety of reasons why people don't delegate—insecurity, fear, selfishness, and outright poor management skills. As a result they waste their resources and those of the business for which they work. When you delegate, be sure to give the authority commensurate with the responsibility and provide accountability structures for completion of the task.
- Focus on your responsibilities by asking, "What is there in this project that only I can do?" Answer this question to define what you will take on, and delegate the rest.
- Schedule and lead efficient meetings.
  - » When a person requests a meeting, ask how you might help them deal with their issue then and there. This might save forty-five to sixty minutes in a meeting.
  - » State a start and end time for every meeting. Be as punctual in ending as you are in beginning. Toward the end time you can say, "Our time is about up, what else do we need to accomplish in these last few minutes?"
  - » Choose which meetings to attend and which meetings to call. Get the right people in the right meetings and include only those necessary to the discussion.
  - » Use an agenda. If non-agenda items surface, be respectful of others and assign those items to another agenda.
  - » Be prepared. Carefully prepare needed information in advance of the meeting. Keep the discussion on track and to the point. Summarize discussions, clarify major points, and assign follow-through responsibilities and deadlines. People appreciate an efficiently run meeting that controls the agenda, time use, and the talkers.

» **Life without regret requires managing priorities to live according to your definition of self, values, vocation, mission, and vision.** Life without regret requires continuing to clarify your boundaries and developing skills in assertiveness and priority management. This takes discipline, reflection, interaction with others, and practice. Be gracious and compassionate to yourself when you get off track, and celebrate every achievement of protecting and working toward "first things first."

Faith Sticky Note: First Things

There are so many things that can become "first things." The question of priorities is answered by clear identification of your definition of self, values, vocation, mission, and vision.

Because of my faith there is only one really big first thing, and that is following my calling from God to seek and serve His kingdom. This calling informs my value choices, my vocation, my personal mission statement, and my vision for life. I live this out in light of my definition of self—strengths, personality, gifts, talents, and styles. Having a "really big first thing" brings great order and less confusion to living.

Problems come when I make something else the priority or allow something to slip into a place of priority it does not deserve. Without a central focus, I tend get things out of order. Problems also come when I work outside of who I am, my definition of self.

Even when I make choices in light of my definition of self, values, vocation, mission, and vision, I use other filters as well in determining priorities. Here are a few questions I find helpful in further sharpening the focus of my life and creating priorities:

- Which of these is most likely to have positive results that will endure beyond my life?
- What will contribute most to the betterment of my life and that of others?

- Which of the choices has the greatest potential impact on eternity?

What will you keep in a priority position? For a free presentation with more on managing priorities go to www.DiscoverYourTrueCourse.com/readerbonus and download the "Do More that Matters" webinar.

Chapter 10

Perfectionism and Regret

Imperfections are not inadequacies;
they are reminders that we're all in this together.

— Brené Brown

"I am a recovering perfectionist." These were the opening words I wrote for an autobiographical paper required for my Doctor of Ministry degree. I was thirty-five and had experienced much of the fallout that generally follows perfectionism. What I once thought was an asset now felt more like a curse.

My field supervisor was the head of the behavioral sciences department at a local university, an experienced pastor, and a very capable sociologist. Using a tone that seemed to question the wisdom of such an idea, he asked, "Why would you want to be that?"

I responded that my perfectionistic approach to life and work had not served me well. As I continued my retrospective account, I recalled thoughts and actions I once believed represented giving 110 percent and doing the best that could be done—superior work. Indeed my thoughts and actions were all these things, but I had come to realize that they were over-the-top perfectionistic behaviors. I also recalled the pain that I allowed perfectionism to create for me.

I came to recognize that I could either take action to avoid regret or I could continue to set myself up for it with my perfectionistic approach to life. Later in this chapter I'll recount the rest of this interaction, which changed me forever.

Perfectionistic tendencies can torpedo your ability to live without regret. Your standards are so unreasonably high that you are continually disappointed and create one regret after another. They can also make you avoid getting started on projects, and when you do get started, you never finish them for fear they will be less than perfect.

Who?

You know the perfectionist. It may be you—the neatly groomed, well-organized, competent, confident, "seems to have it all together" person who is driven to do extremely well. You might throw away a large stack of fliers because a period is missing at the end of a paragraph. You might feel like what you achieve is never good enough. When it comes to projects, you wait until the last minute to start and then spend too much time working on them, or you put off starting even longer because you are anxious to get them just right. You feel that you must give 110 percent and more to what you do or you will be mediocre or even a failure.

Inside, perfectionists are highly critical and seldom, if ever, satisfied. They are often insecure, distrustful, fearful of failure, fearful of making mistakes, and fearful of disapproval, and feel forever inadequate. Perfectionists often feel much false guilt and real shame. After a perfectionist fails over and over to achieve their standard of perfection, pessimism comes to rule their perspective. They believe they are worthless if not perfect in their being and doing.

The way they feel about themselves is based on how they believe others judge them. They think, "If my appearance or my product is perfect, then no one can criticize me or think little of me."

Perfectionists usually hold their ideal as a standard for themselves and for others, and believe that others hold it for them. They believe that to be okay they must achieve perfection in any or all of the areas of personal appearance, skill, and production. They expect the same in others, and when others fall short, they are often excessively critical and push others harder to achieve the goal. They believe others expect them to be perfect, and often sense external pressure to do so. Perfectionists live with a constant sense of failure in measuring up, and believe others are evaluating them critically and continually.

What Is It?

Perfectionism is a product of nature and nurture. Those who feel compelled to be perfect have learned to find their value in what they achieve and in others' approval of what they achieve. Perfectionism can be linked to obsessive-compulsive disorder (OCD). In fact, some who obsess about having their "ducks in a row" describe themselves or aspects of their behavior as OCD rather than perfectionism.

Perfectionism is insidious in that one can hold it as a virtuous way of being. Society applauds many of its qualities. But in reality it can be a miserable, self-defeating, disappointing, and depressing way of living. It can actually freeze you out of the achievement and success you really want.

No one is to blame for your or my perfectionism. At some point you chose it as a way to approach life. However, contributions to this way of being often start in childhood.

My father died in 1993 at the age of sixty-seven. He is more of a giant to me today than ever. At his funeral, a large high school auditorium was packed and overflowing into the foyer with people whose lives he had deeply touched.

I know my father loved me and always wanted great things for me. He did the finest job of parenting he could possibly do. But things were rarely good enough for him.

I was also privileged to know my grandfather (the farmer, my father's father), and he had high expectations as well. I am the first-born in my family, and I caught the bug. I come by it honestly.

I don't blame either of these giants in my family for my perfectionism. I own it. I do believe they influenced it. I nurtured it for a long time.

I believe some religious circles are also incubators for perfectionism. Their espoused belief is salvation by grace through faith alone. But their belief-in-use appears to be that failure in perfectly following religious precept is evidence of spiritual alienation from God. Such an environment engenders perfectionistic thinking and behavior that is far away from grace. Your perfectionism might be influenced by your religious background.

Blessing and a Curse

It's generally a good thing to have high standards and work hard. But perfectionism takes these two good qualities to an unachievable, unhealthy level. **In fact, perfectionism can live along a continuum from helpful to** unhelpful and even destructive. **My personal opinion is that perfection-ism always leads to failed expectations, disappointment, and the pain of regret.**

Perfectionistic tendencies can be helpful when they motivate a person to reach their goals while experiencing pleasure in doing so—and if the person is able to adapt psychologically to the failure when they fall short of perfect. I want my surgeon, dentist, and air traffic controller to be a lit-tle perfectionistic. But even these people need to go easy on themselves and others when they are not in the operating room or the control tower. If they instead apply their perfectionistic standard both in an out of the role in which it helps motivate them, it can become a problem for them and those around them.

Perfectionism is unhelpful and can even be destructive when it drives a person to work toward an unreasonable or unobtainable ideal; if they fall short of perfect they can experience psychological distress—stress due to pressure to perform, tension, sadness, anger, or fear of embar-rassment.

Here's the truth: Most people do not notice others' efforts to make things "perfect." And they don't notice most of the "imperfections" ei-ther.

Dealing with Perfectionism

One of my degrees is in choral music education. I am also an accom-plished, though rusty, percussionist. My years in music school only ex-acerbated my perfectionism, since in music the pitch is the pitch, the rhythm is the rhythm, and anything else is incorrect. Though there is a correct/incorrect nature to music, there is also much that is subjective and highly dependent on the listener. Try chasing perfection with that! No teacher called for my personal best, only better.

Maestro Benjamin Zander tells of his approach to helping students take risks, work toward excellence, and be psychologically healthy at the same time. In his work with musicians, the environment can be tense be-cause they are competitors and can be pretty hard on themselves. **When a student in his orchestra makes a mistake, they are required to lift their arms in the air and say, "How fascinating!" This helps loosen things up**

and put the mistake in perspective. The mistake takes on potential by becoming a learning opportunity.[10] You might try this tactic some time for yourself and those you love.

I continue to learn the importance of striving for excellence rather than perfection. Even as I write this I want to achieve what is truly excellent for me rather than the perfection I might try to achieve in order to defend myself against criticism.

I have also come to recognize that most of my work does not require, nor can it wait for, what I might consider perfect. There is a need for expediency *and* excellence. Getting the job done in a timely and excellent fashion is more important than getting it done perfectly.

When approaching a task, I am also helped by reframing the situation by asking, "Will additional improvement matter? Will making this better than it is right now matter tomorrow? Next week? Next year? In ten years?" If the answer to any of these is no, then I release it.

When tempted by perfectionism, ask yourself, "What is driving me to work on improving my work [appearance, etc.]? Is it fear? Is it to help me feel better about me? Is it to protect myself from criticism?"

What should you do when perfectionism creates more regret than help?

- **See a good therapist.** Allow them to help you identify your beliefs about perfectionism, determine if it really makes sense to hold on to perfectionistic beliefs, and make a strong determination about whether or not it really achieves what you want.
- **Adopt a standard of excellence** rather than perfection.
- **Decide what you want to achieve in a time period.** Cut that back to 80 percent. Your 80 percent likely equals the 150 percent of others' efforts, and you will cut yourself some deserved slack in the process.
- **Determine when to pronounce a task "done."** Perfectionism keeps you working on the task well past "done" to the point of counter-productivity.
- **Accept failure.** Embrace the fact that you can learn more from failure than from success. I often say that those who work hard to make a C in my classes probably learn more than those who make an A. Thomas A. Edison was known to believe that in every failure he learned one more way not to do a thing; with each failure he was getting closer to the way of doing what he wanted. Just imagine what we would have lost if he'd

been paralyzed by regret over every failure.

- **Enjoy the journey.** When drowning in perfectionism it is virtually impossible to enjoy the journey; the journey is secondary. Elevate it to the level of achievement. If you are journeying and contributing, that's achievement.
- **Embrace feedback and constructive criticism.** Now, I admit, this can be like hugging a cactus, but get up your courage, listen, and ask the person to explain more about what they are saying to you.
- **Be open to gray.** Perfectionists are often black-and-white thinkers. Open yourself to the possibilities of gray when it is appropriate and does not violate your moral standards.
- **Celebrate when you complete a task,** pass a milestone, or achieve a goal, no matter how small. Celebration need not be a giant party. It can be taking time to treat yourself to something you enjoy while basking in completion. Give yourself a pat on the back—literally.
- **Let your support team** help you.
- **Take baby steps.** Recognize that you will not always deal with perfectionism perfectly. Baby steps are valuable and a great way to start.

My hope for you is that you can extend appreciation, grace, and compassion to yourself as you plan to live without regret, all of which you may believe is undeserved. Use the principles in Chapter 14 and create a powerful team to support you in dealing with perfectionism. Include a counselor and a coach on your team. You'll be happier, healthier, and on your way to living without regret.

After I tried to explain to my field supervisor about the merits of being "a recovering perfectionist," I discovered that he was playing the devil's advocate and driving me even deeper into thought and reflection (which made him a great supervisor, by the way). He related how he had come to manage his own perfectionistic tendencies. Regardless of your faith tradition, I hope this is helpful to you. He said something along these lines:

> I look into the first few chapters of Genesis in the Christian Scriptures and note that God, who is perfection in His being and all His ways, chose to create. After each period of creation, Scripture says He viewed His work as "good" or "very good." Notice that He did not create it as "perfect." I have taken that to mean that God saw

what He created as "good enough." I believe that if God, who is perfect and could create perfection, can create something that is "good enough" and be pleased with it, I can do that, too.

After sharing this story with driven high-achievers who are often perfectionistic, I ask questions such as, "What would it be like for you to pronounce your work as good enough? Your appearance good enough? Your product good enough? Your colleagues good enough? Your spouse good enough? Your children good enough?"

You may not feel or think "good enough" when you pronounce it. You need to be like a law court judge, pound the gavel, and forensically pronounce your efforts "good enough" even though those perfectionistic tendencies call for still more.

Martha is a driven, incredibly high achiever who was living in crippling fear of falling short and embarrassing herself in front of a crowd. Her performance and appearance were never good enough. This created a type of stage fright that robbed her of joy in her job performance. The pressure of this led to Martha taking up a couple of undesirable, potentially self-destructive habits. When she began to pronounce her performance and appearance as "good enough," the tension began to relax, she began to see life more clearly and appreciate the little things more, and she got control of those undesirable habits. She describes the "good enough" idea as nothing short of life-changing transformation.

I hope you will experience this, too.

Faith Sticky Note: **Whole and Complete**

Only God is perfect, fully complete, and whole. He did not place the quality of perfection into you or me or anything else in His creation. His creation is imperfect, but He described it as "good."

He put freedom of choice into the scheme of creation. With this freedom we clearly demonstrate our own imperfection. We are by nature bent toward destruction of self, others, and the whole of creation.

God's standard for us—what He wants—is that our lives be abundant and eternal. He does not want us to think and act in ways that hurt us, others, or Him. When we are involved in such, it hurts Him. His anger is directed toward such behavior and its effects. Our imperfections and destructive behaviors alienate us from God.

As an expression of His grace—favor undeserved—God goes an extra mile with us. He has made a way to deal with the effects of our imperfection and a way to lovingly deal with our imperfections and destructive nature through the sacrificial work of His son, Jesus Christ, and bring us back into relationship with Him.

We need not be perfect. We need the perfect one and the forgiveness He provides by grace through faith in Christ. We need not be perfect, just forgiven. We need not be perfect, but to choose His work to produce eternal and abundant life in us and for us.

Chapter 11

Self-Care for Life without Regrets

*To observe the "discipline of living in the present moment" is to accept
one's present situation and find satisfaction and peace in the now.
This is distinguished from attitudes of restlessness and dissatisfaction,
worry about the future or discouragement and regret about the past.
By trusting in God now and allowing the present to be enjoyed,
greater happiness and peace is possible.*

—Jean-Pierre de Caussade

Information overload and hectic, busy schedules can make life feel like trying to drink from a fire hose. We can let them distract us, push us around, overwhelm us, and drain energy reserves in all aspects of our being, leaving us without essential resources to be, see, and achieve what matters to us. This is a clear path to regret. Instead we can determine to take extreme action to care for ourselves so we have reserves (not leftovers) to offer ourselves and others.

False Beliefs about Self-Care

"I'd rather burn out than rust out." Actually, neither of these is desirable. The desirable state is a sharp, well-managed, well-cared-for self, marked by highly polished excellence.

"Others first." I appreciate this sentiment and firmly believe that we are to care for others and their needs in appropriate ways. But if we care for others too much, to the neglect of our own health and well-being, we become unable to care for anyone.

"Care for self is selfish." Some think that giving attention to care of self or any attention to self at all is somehow selfish and evidence of a lack of spiritual commitment, and may be bad, immoral, or sinful. But there is a difference between caring for self and being selfish. Selfishness implies a kind of self-centeredness that cares only for one's self, interests, and

welfare. Self-care is responsible management of our own being, which allows us to be strong and healthy for making a difference in the world.

"Less than full is normal." Some individuals live with their personal energy indicator (physical, emotional, spiritual, mental, social) chronically on "D" (for drained). They may get stuck on D because they pronounce "less than full" on energy to be normal. For example, when we reach three-quarters full, we can become accustomed to running at three-quarters full and unconsciously declare that to be the new full level. If after a while we reach one-half full and repeat the process with one-half as the new full, and so forth until we hit D for drained, we wonder how we got there. Pay attention to your own being. Be vigilant. Know what 100 percent full feels like and do what is necessary to continue filling the tank.

My Crash

I was thirty-one years old and leading a large youth ministry at a local church. We were working toward one of the largest youth events in our area before or since. I was also preparing to begin doctoral studies the following January. My son was four and my daughter was twenty months old.

In November we sponsored a speaker at seventeen area schools, literally leap-frogging multiple sound systems from school to school over a three-day period. There were nightly meetings as well. On the final night we gathered 4,000 students for music, a speaker, and pizza. An army of people made this possible.

As the event closed very successfully and with high acclaim, pain I was experiencing in my back became more prominent. After very extensive medical testing, no physical problems were found.

Then, during December, I began to experience what I now know was clinical depression and panic attacks. I had pushed too hard, too far, too fast. Every aspect of my being was shouting at me. My functioning and productivity was impaired. I had bottomed out.

I continued to move forward with my doctoral studies, still depressed and panicky, studying intensely from mid-December through February, including one month of sixteen-hour days in residency on campus. I also officiated at my brother's wedding in the midst of my residency.

I am not one to let problems continue without being addressed. From the time I experienced the first symptoms, I sought care. It took several months for me to understand exactly what was happening. After finding the right therapist and months of therapy and heavy-duty self-care, I gradually improved.

You could call all this "too bad" or "regrettable." But it is not so for me. I learned so much during this difficult time that has benefitted me and others. I now think and behave in a markedly different way and take much better care of myself. I learned that I could live with a level of stress for a time until it felt normal. I could go to the next level until it became the new normal, and then repeat the process... until the top blew off. I learned what it is like to be clinically depressed, chronically anxious, and even panicky for a time. I am still learning from that experience, and because of it I am able to better coach highly driven executives who are living on the edge of what I experienced or floundering in it.

Ebb and Flow

In *The Making of a Corporate Athlete*, Tony Schwartz and Jim Loehr suggest that high performance involves the whole of self—physical, emotional, mental, and spiritual (and I think *social* belongs in there somewhere). They suggest that peak performance is possible as we create rituals and routines that allow us to "oscillate" into activity (flow = expending energy) and out of activity (ebb = rest and recovery). Expend/recover rituals are vitally important.[11]

For example, I am a somewhat introverted individual. Being with too many people too much drains my energy. An excessively fast pace of life or an extended busy schedule drains me. When I must be with people intensively or carry a busier schedule, I must also plan to rest to build reserves prior to the demands and to rest to recover afterward. One of my rituals is napping. You might say, "Sleep when you are dead." I say, "If I don't sleep I will be dead, and if you cross me before I've recovered..." Well, you get the meaning, I think.

We need the ebb and flow cycle in every area of our being. Some habits I've found to be important for me might be helpful for you:

Physical Self-Care

- Exercise regularly.
- Eat healthy foods.
- Achieve an ideal weight and body mass index. Specialists in this area say portion control is the key. Join a weight-loss program if that works for you.
- See your physician at least once yearly.
- Practice good sleep hygiene. Do what is necessary to sleep well in quantity and quality. Seven to eight hours' sleep per day is optimal. For help with consistently getting a renewing, refreshing night's sleep, go to www.DiscoverYourTrueCourse.com/readerbonus and download your free tips.
- Breathe more deeply more often. This helps you relax and oxygenates your brain.
- Drink more water. Sixty-four ounces per day is still the standard. If you drink this much, you will get some of your exercise from going to the bathroom.
- Stand up more. Sitting is killing you. Use a desk arrangement that allows you to sit or stand.
- For Type A personalities:
  - » Plan to use only 80 percent of your day. Leave the other 20 percent for emergencies and putting out fires. If you don't have emergencies and fires on a given day, use the time to get ahead.
  - » Learn to intentionally relax using specialized relaxation techniques or other activities that are calming for you.
  - » If you have difficulty getting going on these, hire a trainer or coach to help you with goals and accountability.

Emotional Self-Care

- Get plenty of rest and relaxation. Do what it takes to feel rested and relaxed.
- Laugh and smile more. The physical act of smiling has an emotional impact. Go ahead; smile right now and hold it. See if you don't feel better.
- Go on a news fast. You will feel better emotionally if you do. If a nuclear holocaust happens, someone will let you know.
- Serve another person not related to your job. Recently my neighbor's

wife was diagnosed with cancer and they had to be away from their home for lengthy periods of time. It was my privilege to care for their yard while they were away, which was totally unrelated to my job. This was emotionally nurturing for me and helpful for them.

- Forgive moment by moment.
- Try solitude. Get alone, get still—physically and mentally, and see what comes up inside you.
- Avoid negative people and those who drain you. Love, help, and do your best to serve others, but avoid these draining influences.
- Be ruthlessly grateful and hopeful. Before I get out of bed in the morning, I try to identify several things for which I am grateful and several things for which I am hopeful, and to pronounce things as "enough." I do all in my power to replace any negative thought that surfaces with things for which I am grateful and hopeful.
- Focus on speaking to yourself with love, kindness, grace, and compassion.
- Talk about your feelings. If you have a need to talk about your feelings, be sure to engage your support team and other safe individuals for this purpose.
- Be emotionally and socially aware and adept. Work on increasing your awareness of your own thoughts and emotions and your sensitivity to the emotions of others. Grow in your ability to self-manage, self-regulate, and skillfully interact in light of your emotions, personality, personal style, and relational style, and those of others.

Mental Self-Care

It's important to acknowledge that thinking is one of the most intensive energy-users of all our activities. Pacing and caring for yourself mentally is essential. Schedule blocks of time so that you're fresh for different types of thinking:

- Critical thinking. Involves analysis.
- Organizing and planning. Prioritizing tasks and activities requires the most intensive use of mental energy. Schedule this work at the time of day when you sense you are usually fresh and alert.
- Synthesizing. Gathering concepts and ideas to form an integrated whole.
- Creative thinking. Developing new, novel, innovative ideas.

- Intuitive thinking. Sensing or perceiving truth without empirical evidence and incorporating it into the whole of an idea or decision. This includes non-Western and somatic ways of knowing (also known as gut feelings).

When you have trouble thinking clearly or productively, don't try harder; take a break. Schwartz and Loehr encourage us to seek recovery every 90 to 120 minutes through "five sources of restoration: eat something, hydrate, move physically, change channels mentally, and change channels emotionally."[12]

Your overall health impacts your mental energy. Mental capacity and performance is built primarily on the foundation of physical capability, and secondarily on emotional capacity. If either of these two foundational capacities is weak, mental capacity and performance is limited.[13]

Spiritual Self-Care

Spiritual health is described differently according to your spiritual background and religious tradition. Some of the following work for everyone regardless of their spiritual orientation. Others come from my Christian religious tradition.

- Take time personally to simply *be* versus *do*. This means you might take that time just to be with God versus performing some discipline.
- Use silence and stillness as a discipline.
- Meditate. This can include prayer and meditation on religious writings.
- Be quick to acknowledge sin to God.
- Use a spiritual formation approach that is compatible with your personality rather than a one-size-fits-all approach. The indicator about whether your approach is effective comes with the answer to the question "Are you being formed and growing spiritually?"
- Stay focused on your calling or vocation, on who you are and why you are here, and on your most important values. Getting your eyes up and off of the rat race of life and reflecting on the deeper and broader aspects of life are spiritually nurturing.

Resilience

As you pursue extreme self-care, cultivate the quality that will help you bounce back from difficulty and challenge: Resilience.

In her excellent book, *The Gifts of Imperfection*, Dr. Brené Brown, a shame researcher and sociology professor at the University of Houston, summarizes the common qualities of resilient people as:

- Resourcefulness
- Good problem-solving skills
- More likely to seek help than the less resilient
- Belief that they can do something to manage their feelings and cope
- Connected to social support and people such as family and friends
- Possessors of shared and deeply held beliefs.[14]

You will discover that every item mentioned in this chapter contributes to one or more of these items suggested by Dr. Brown. If you faithfully practice the principles of extreme self-care outlined in this chapter, you will likely become one of the most resilient people on the planet and set yourself up for a life without regret.

Creating Reserves

Creating reserves in the physical, emotional, social, mental, and spiritual areas of your life can keep you from being in survival mode and help you rise to the occasion when draining challenges come. Reserves establish options and choice. You need much more of a reserve in each of these areas than you might believe. To create physical, emotional, social, mental, and spiritual reserves:

- Commit to doing it and make it a top priority.
- Practice extreme self-care even when you don't think or feel you need to do so.
- Observe and assess your current levels of reserve or deficit. Write this out on paper for each of the five categories.
- Imagine what you would sense when you have great reserves in the five categories. (How will it look? What will it sound like? What will it feel like?)
- Keep in mind that you will need more reserves than you think.
- Try to make what you just imagined measurable. Create benchmarks for measurement.
- Create a list of ideas for extreme self-care practices for each of the categories.

- Begin creating a natural, workable extreme self-care routine. Start with baby steps. Choose one simple routine for each of the five categories to start. Add from there.
- Do what is needed to remind you to engage in your self-care routine until it becomes habit. If necessary put it on your calendar and/or task list or a wall poster.
- Continue to develop your routine by adding self-care activities as needed and make them reasonable and effective for building reserves.
- When the routine is in place, just relax and work the routine.

Burnout

If you don't practice the principles of extreme self-care, you could well be headed for burnout. Some thinking, actions, and conditions that pave the way to burnout are:

- Physical exhaustion
- Withdrawal and detachment from people
- Boredom and cynicism
- Elevated impatience and irritability
- Sense of omnipotence: "Nobody can do my job better than me."
- Feelings of being unappreciated
- Change of work style—withdrawing or becoming more demanding or inflexible
- Paranoia
- Disorientation and wandering thought processes
- Psychosomatic complaints
- Depression
- Suicidal thinking

Burnout has mental/emotional symptoms, physical symptoms, and spiritual symptoms that look much like what brought a person to burnout to begin with. **If "burnout" describes you, take the first opportunity to consult a good therapist or counselor.** Once you have done this, start creating routines to live out the extreme self-care practices above. You'll create a greater sense of balance and begin to heal. You'll be glad you did and you'll be moving to a life without regret.

Faith Sticky Note: **Self First?**

I believe that everything belongs to God. He entrusts some of it to our care. This includes the totality of our being—breath, the beat of the heart, energy, and capacity. All belong to God, not us. And He expects that we manage their use for His glory.

When we wreck our health in any area of our being, we give sorry management to the other things with which He has entrusted us, including relationships. We are responsible for managing ourselves. This allows us to take effective action for extreme care of God's gifts.

So when we care for ourselves, we are more likely to be able to care for others. Extreme self-care can translate into extreme care for others.

Chapter 12

If You Do This, Expect Conflict

*Whenever you're in conflict with someone, there is one factor
that can make the difference between damaging your relationship
and deepening it. That factor is attitude.*

—William James

If you have done these things...
- Completed your work of self-definition; established your values, vocation, purpose, and vision; and drawn boundaries
- Committed yourself to all of the above
- Taken action on these commitments

...then conflict has also been a part of your experience. I guarantee it.

Conflict can range from a simple difference of opinion or a problem to solve—healthy conflict, to all-out war—which is, of course, unhealthy conflict. When the focus of conflict moves from the issue and becomes personal, regret is close at hand.

Let me show you the way to manage conflict so that things turn out in the best way possible and you don't put out the welcome mat for regret in your life.

The Myth of Conflict Resolution

I flinch when I hear the phrase *conflict resolution*. In my conflict management classes I tell students, "I don't believe conflict can be resolved, nor should it be." Their response: Silence. Mouths open and brows furrow.

Even those who agree about most things have some disagreement on the finer points of an issue. This is conflict. Thus, where two or three are gathered, even in the healthiest contexts, there will be conflict at some level. When it appears that conflict is "resolved," further probing into the thoughts and emotions of those involved reveals that conflict remains. It's just gone underground and needs to be managed. **Without some low-level conflict, relationships and organizations are depressed, angry, unhealthy, and unproductive.**

When referring to working with conflict, I prefer the term *conflict management.* We manage conflict by creating and participating in an environment that respectfully appreciates others' opinions, allowing them to hold to those opinions while holding to ours with integrity.

Learning to manage productive conflict between individuals and in groups helps you achieve life without regret.

Conflict Management Styles

In my informal research regarding how people manage conflict I've discovered that just a tiny percentage run excitedly to the battle.

Most would rather stay home and avoid it at all costs. They consider conflict to be bad, difficult, and destructive, and to be avoided at all costs (yes, all). Avoiders take the ostrich approach to conflict by placing their heads in the sand and hoping conflict will go away.

And then there are all the styles in between that persuade, force, ignore, flee, accommodate, collaborate, or negotiate.

Conflict Is Good

Not long after that first statement about conflict, I tell my students, "I believe conflict is a good thing." Then their faces show real confusion. I'm sure they think I'm losing (or have already lost) my mind. Though conflict can escalate to a level that is destructive and can create fertile ground for regret, a certain level of conflict is very healthy, constructive, and worthy of embrace.

Conflict is good when the focus is on an issue such as solving a problem or settling a disagreement. My wife and I have been married since 1976. Sometimes we fail to clearly understand one another's words, thoughts, or intentions. This produces conflict. We have differences of opinion about schedules, finances, and priorities that produce conflict. We have determined, however, to make our conflicts about *issues* and not about one another. Because of this, we have spirited discussions that help us grow together and individually. This is good conflict. Settling a disagreement can involve seeking consensus (agreeing enough to move forward) or agreeing to disagree and walking away with a good, respectful personal relationship and a win/win solution.

The best problem-solving requires that everyone place their opinions on the table and that each opinion be respected and valued by others (though they may not agree). Healthy, energetic collaboration using contributions from each person can sift out a better answer than any individual could have achieved on their own. In such settings we are wise to hold and communicate our own opinions, but to hold them loosely lest we miss a learning opportunity.

Argument is an important part of managing conflict. In fact, it is a classic skill that involves very calculated, respectful, and orderly debate, and has been the birthplace of many of the ideologies, theologies, ethical stances, and philosophies that guide our lives and social interactions.

Because people often get anxious during arguments and let their behavior get out of hand, the term *argument* has come to refer to an undesirable, ill-mannered, and, at times, unruly interaction. As children we are admonished, "Don't argue; that's not nice" or "Don't argue with me." When we hear the words "they had an argument" in reference to a relationship, this often means that shouting and strong words were involved and the discussion became more than a simple difference of opinion. It's no wonder our first inclination is to avoid arguing about differences of opinion lest we be frowned upon.

My wife and I, however, taught our children that they were free to disagree with us if they were respectful in doing so. And they took the opportunity.

Conflict is good because it creates opportunities to learn new things. It can be unsettling to encounter an opinion that is different from yours about something important. But this unsettling experience shakes you out of a very comfortable frame of mind and into a learning one. When your confidence in your opinion is shaken, what you previously believed does not make as much sense as it once did. This discomfort creates a need to learn in order to restore a sense of equilibrium. You explore ways to reorient around ideas you can live with and which make more sense.

Conflict is good because it can help you gain understanding of the give-and-take skills needed for living in community with others, and sharpen these skills. Personality and style differences are not bad or necessarily born of ill will, but they can be fertile ground for conflict. In such conflict, you can learn to be with people who have strengths and styles that are very different from yours, and come to appreciate their contributions to the world. This alone helps you live your life without regret.

This was illustrated in one of my conflict management classes. Most in the class were introverted, reflective, and thought carefully before speaking. Some were people-oriented, but liked to choose who to be with, when, and how much. Then Lance joined the class. He was extremely outgoing, energetic, forthright, and task-oriented. He processed his thoughts aloud. When Lance spoke I could see the rest of the class grow tense as their eyes went down to the tables, avoiding eye contact with him. Not one engaged him in argument or discussion. One day Lance engaged me in a direct confrontation in front of the class. You could have heard a pin drop.

When I had my students complete the Birkman® personality assessment, they realized that Lance's style and theirs (and mine) were on opposite ends of the spectrum. Therein was the source of discomfort. One class member told me, "When Lance showed up, I thought you had planted him as a way to teach the rest of us about managing conflict." The class realized that Lance wasn't a jerk, being cocky, or trying to be "smart." His style was just different from theirs. They began to open up to Lance and engage in dialogue with him more. Their body language was much more relaxed when Lance spoke.

When Conflict Is Bad

Conflict is bad when the situation escalates to a win/lose battle and people are attacked while the issues become secondary and unclear. People with an alternate opinion are characterized as wrong and marginalized from the mainstream. Character assassination is common, and in relatively rare cases, physical assassination. The goal becomes the elimination of the individual from the scene. Thus relationships are broken and cut off, and the original issue remains unaddressed. We can disagree without regret, but when people are attacked and hurt, regret is much more likely.

What the Brain Is Up To in Conflict

Recall from Chapter 6 that anxiety involves the reactive reptilian part of your brain. This part of the brain is the source of the fight, flight, or freeze reaction and kicks in when we sense a threat. It's essential to our survival but not helpful for civil and thoughtful interaction. Most conflict is reptilian (reactive and not thinking), especially when it's focused on a person.

Planning, analysis, and decision-making happen in the cerebral cortex—your higher, thinking brain. When conflict includes healthy disagreement, difference of opinion, and problem-solving, the rational cerebral cortex is still at work creatively, thinking through options with dashes of anxiety here and there. Thought is needed for conflict management, preserving relationships, and moving projects forward.

But if everyone in the conflict is anxious and reactive, no one is thinking. You've been in conflicts in which no amount of reasoning will help; you can only reason when the rational cerebral cortex is sufficiently engaged.

Planning to Manage Conflict

Low levels of conflict between people are natural, normal, and inevitable, though sometimes uncomfortable. Expect this and embrace it. You can keep the conflict good and productive when you manage it masterfully.

You can't plan conflict management strategies in a heated, anxious, irrational situation of conflict. Planning how you will be and what you will do to manage conflict involves proactive planning during quiet, non-anxious, rational times.

Your Foundations and Conflict

Not every issue is worthy of argument. What is worth advocating and defending to you?

Your conflict management strategy has its roots in your personal foundations. Your foundations determine what you will argue and how you will treat people and things in the process. This includes your definitions of your:

- Self – who you are in the core of your being and how you are different from others
- Values – that which is most important to you
- Vocation – your calling
- Mission – your perceived highest reason for being
- Vision – what you hope to accomplish in the future
- Boundaries – how you relate to others

About Others in the Conflict

- Other parties in the conflict are not under your control.
- Others parties in the conflict might be anxious and irrational. Do not intensify this by being the same way.
- All people are whole, capable, competent, and sincere in their opinions. Respect them.

In *Leading through Conflict: How Successful Leaders Transform Differences into Opportunities*, Mark Gerzon explains important concepts for leading through conflict. Some of his ideas are incorporated into the information below.[15]

About Conflict Processes

- Understand how people, opinions, processes, and the conflict at hand are related (including you and yours).
- Balance advocacy and inquiry. Ask questions to understand the other viewpoint. Calmly and rationally advocate for your principles.
- Argue on principle versus position. The key question leading to productive conflict is "What is it that we all want out of this?" Areas of agreement discovered are the foundation for moving forward together. A most desirable outcome is that everyone gets something they wanted: win/win.
- Communicate as objectively as possible, with trust and vulnerability. The goal of communicating in conflict is to build connections that reach

through the conflict to find new ways to create consensus and work toward productive ends for conflict.

- Use dialogue. Dialogue involves mutual respect for the differences involved, not trying to convince the other person to change to suit you, and not changing to suit them. It involves hearing meaning clearly, without the filters of our own biases; seeking understanding; respecting opinions; and learning to live with the tension.
- Create space. When the situation is too anxious to be productive, request a break or schedule another time to discuss the matter. This can diffuse the anxiety. It's like counting to ten when you're angry. Set a time and try again.

About Ideas, Issues, Opinions, and Conflict
- Keep in mind that your thinking might not be right after all. There might not be a right or wrong. Stay open and be willing to learn.
- Opinions can be characterized as valuable, valid, or both. An opinion can be valuable as a window for solving a problem, or it might create a viable approach to an issue but not be completely valid. *Valid* means the opinion is well-founded and sound; not all opinions are. Cultivate the viewpoint that even if the opinion seems not valid for the moment, it is valuable and respectable because the person holding it is valuable and respectable.

About You and Conflict
- You are a part of the conflict; it takes two to tango.
- Self-manage the whole of your being to engage the many options for your behavior in conflict.
- Do what you decide, not what you feel. Your gut will say "fight," "take flight," or "freeze." This is natural and normal. But instead, gently lean into the conversation, embrace the situation, and ask questions to aid you in understanding what the other person wants. Relax your hands, sit back, uncross your arms, relax your shoulders and your facial muscles, and listen. You need not rush to make a statement. But do speak. Put ideas out there and take baby steps to engage in conversation.
- A quiet (not whispering), well-paced voice can help you and others be calmer and project calmness into the otherwise anxious situation.

- Be a calm, rational (thinking, non-reactive, non-anxious) presence who is actively processing the interaction. When you are thinking, not reacting, you can help others think more and react less.
- An essential tactic in being a calm, rational presence in conflict is to intentionally breathe deeply from your belly. Inhale deeply through your nose, pushing your belly out. Then exhale through your mouth. Practice this outside of conflict situations.
- In conflict, concentrate on your breathing until you sense you are gaining control of yourself. This gives you more access to your thinking brain because you are consciously, intentionally enacting a plan. You need not make a show of breathing deeply. Breathe quietly and discretely as you listen to the other person.
- Maintain the heart of a respectful learner, not a manipulator or a patronizer.
- Stay focused on the issues. Don't make the conflict about the other person.
- Be curious. Ask questions that help you fully understand the other position. Require the other person to access their thinking brain to provide an answer. Ask questions such as "What do you hope will come of our conversation?" Or ask, "What more would you like for me to know about that?"
- Be attentive. Listen 80 percent of the time and speak 20 percent of the time. In conflict people say many things, possibly hurtful things, to which you need not respond and from which you need not defend yourself. They are reacting, not thinking. Listening more can help you discover the core of the issue.
- You need not apologize for your ideas and opinions. But if you speak too much or try to defend too much, you might say something you will have to live with but wish you didn't. This can lead to regret.
- Be open and vulnerable. Openness and vulnerability is often disarming and helpful in conflict. This is counterintuitive, since in conflict we naturally tend to erect walls and be protective.
- Be assertive. Use the assertiveness techniques from Chapter 8. Stick to the "I" messages and avoid accusing or blaming. Speak only for yourself and not others.
- Embrace silence. Silence and breathing deeply gives the thinking brain room to engage.

J. Michael Godfrey

Faith Sticky Note: **Conflict in the Bible?**

The Apostle Paul's Philippian letter is mostly joyful and celebratory in its tone. But evidently there had been a loss of focus and conflict had arisen in his church. When any group loses clear focus on their common purpose, personal agendas arise and conflict ensues.

To address the conflict, Paul encouraged the church to refocus, be "like-minded" and "intent on one purpose," and look to their common interests—that they would be God's people in the world, His ambassadors, carrying out His loving mission in the world.

He further encouraged them not to be self-centered or conceited but to count others as better than self with humility. This sounds like respect for people and the opinions of others to me.

Chapter 13

Forgive and Forget?

Life is an adventure in forgiveness.
—Norman Cousins

If you live long enough you will experience feelings of regret for having hurt others and having been hurt. Sometimes the hurting is selfish, mean, malicious, and intentional. At other times it is simply a part of bumping up against others as we live in community on this tiny planet.

Whether you are the one who did the hurting or the one who hurts, you cannot cut off and live separately from everyone who hurts you or from those you hurt. Either would constitute a very lonely existence.

At some point, sooner than later, you need forgiveness and to forgive others.

Living without regret requires that you be quick to forgive and to seek forgiveness so that your relationships are healthy, whole, and at peace. With this healthy outlook on forgiveness, you can approach the end of life with no unfinished business and no regrets for your behavior in relationships.

What Is Forgiveness?

Forgiveness is a choice to free an offender from any punishment from you and view them with grace and compassion without condoning their actions. Your choice to forgive is like a judge presiding over a case in which the defendant was caught red-handed, but legal issues require the judge to dismiss the case. It is a decision to release the defendant even though he or she is guilty. Forgiveness says, "Though you have offended me, I release you from all responsibility to me for the wrong."

When you do not forgive, you continue to hold an offender responsible to you for their offense. You try the case over and over again in the courtroom of your mind, at great expense to you and with no effect on the offender.

Forgiveness is a gift you give to yourself and to others. It's like any other gift; you choose to give it rather than giving it away grudgingly or because you are compelled to do so. Forgiveness does not mean denying the pain of the wrong or the losses incurred as a result of the wrong.

You need not feel like forgiving. You need not be asked for forgiveness. You can make a decision to forgive and act on it.

Can We Forgive and Forget?

We choose to forgive, but can we really forget? And is it even wise to forget?

We tend to remember things that are important to us or that touch us deeply, for good or ill. We readily remember things that can help us move forward to the future, solve future problems, and protect ourselves from threats.

I believe that forgetting a wrong suffered is neither possible nor advisable. Is it wise to forget that a person stole from you in a business transaction? You may forgive, but if you truly forget you can find yourself in business with the same slick individual again. Is it wise to forget that someone verbally abused you? You forgive them for the unkindness and disrespect, but if you forget and continue in the relationship as if nothing happened, they might abuse you again. Keep forgetting and the process will repeat.

I do not believe you must nurture a memory, obsess over it, replay it, or ruminate over it. But when you are hurt deeply, the memory will arise occasionally, prompted by places, objects, people, and experiences. The moment you remember, you can replace the memory with something more pleasant, but you will remember.

At every memory you can ask the question "Have I really forgiven?" Answer by affirming your forgiveness once more and moving your thoughts to something else. Forgiveness is a moment-by-moment experience.

Offended or Hurt Feelings?

Though they may both generate pains of regret, there is a difference between being wronged through a bona fide offense and letting your emotions get the best of you.

A genuine offense happens when someone breaks a moral code, the civil law, or the law of love, or when they violate the rights or person of another. Examples are someone stealing from you, maliciously turning others against you, cheating in a business deal or relationship, speaking unfairly or abusively, or violating you in some way. They wronged you. They need your forgiveness. Hopefully they will seek it. You would be wise to grant it whether they seek it or not.

When someone wrongs you out of their own personality, without malice or ill intent, you might take their behavior personally. They might kindly and firmly draw a boundary and you don't like it. Some examples are when a person:

- Takes a very frank and direct approach to you, but you prefer a more respectful, easy, and warm approach. You feel sad or angry during and after the encounter.
- Forgets to return your phone call, text, or email, and you judge them to be neglectful of you, irresponsible, or spacy. You become frustrated.
- Is withdrawn in order to practice self-care. You are hurt because you believe they are ignoring you.
- Declines your offer of help.

In any of these examples, the person did not wrong you. Rather, they did not meet your expectations and you took their behavior personally, experiencing negative emotions such as anger, sadness, disgust, or feeling wounded in some way. And you expected the other person to be responsible for all this. But they did not make you have these emotions. You chose the emotions. Forgiveness is not needed, nor is it likely to be sought, but you may decide to make the person suffer for not meeting your expectations. And that could leave you open to doing something you regret.

It's better to choose to extend understanding, compassion, and grace to someone who did not wrong you, but whom you simply do not like. If their personality differences create discomfort for you, allow them to be who they are. If they draw boundaries, respect them as you would want your boundaries to be respected.

Ask yourself this question: "Have I really been wronged or am I allowing my emotions to get the best of me (or getting my feelings hurt)?" This road runs both ways, so you can also ask, "Did I wrong them or did they allow their emotions to get the best of them?

Holding Out for Vindication

When wronged, you will likely become angry and want to punish the offender or see them punished in some way. You want the one who wronged you to "get theirs." (If you don't, please check to see if you have a pulse.)

Sometimes we don't forgive, and hang on to the offense hoping we will be vindicated personally or proved right in the matter. In reality, we not only want to be proved right but we want the other person to be proved wrong.

I get calls from individuals who are in trouble at their job and believe they have been wronged. They are angry, depressed, and confused. Their stories take one of two tracks: The individual is offended and chooses to abruptly resign, or they are fired or asked to resign, sometimes very abruptly. In my work with churches, when someone is asked to resign there is frequently a "hush" agreement tied to their severance pay. It goes like this: "If you will sign and honor this agreement to be quiet about your dismissal/resignation, we will provide you with three months' severance pay. If you break the agreement, your severance will be stopped." This is indicative of intrigue, politics, lies, dysfunctional systems, and often injustice. Individuals are wronged and feel regret. They grieve. They want to be vindicated from the lies and injustice. They want the unjust to get theirs.

But they have a choice about their response. They can choose to forgive even though they experienced a bona fide injustice and served as a scapegoat for irresponsible leadership. They will be called on to choose forgiveness again every time they remember the situation.

When People Won't Forgive

Sometimes people just don't want to resolve issues in their relationships or extend forgiveness. Those who know me well can tell you that I have blind spots; I can offend others, and I'm sure I do my fair share of it. Since I am a confident, yet introverted individual, I can be perceived as arrogant, cold, and aloof at times, though this is not my intention. This in itself is offensive to some. When I become aware of a legitimate offense, I am quick to make amends and at least explore whether or not it is a real offense or someone just letting their feelings be hurt.

I served as executive pastor with Senior Pastor George for about two years in a large church. I thought we had a good relationship, though we were not best friends and did not spend time together outside of the workplace. Years after I left that church I discovered that there was some offense or other issue at play which had become personal.

I made every effort to contact George because I wanted the air to be clear between us. I was willing to apologize for any legitimate offense, but it would have helped to know what the issue was. He would not return my phone calls or meet with me. To this day I am unsure of what the issue is. If there is no offense, I'm okay if George just doesn't like me and perhaps got his feelings hurt. I choose, on a moment-by-moment basis, to let this go. This does not make me a saint or better than George. But I know that holding on to issues like this only hurts me.

Forgive Yourself

In the same way that you would forgive others for their offenses, forgive yourself with great mercy and compassion. Some of us tend to be pretty hard on ourselves when we make a mistake or fail. Stop bringing yourself back to court and putting yourself on trial. Replaying the situation and berating yourself won't do any good. Learn from the experience and practice moment-by-moment forgiveness of yourself as well.

Take Initiative to Forgive

When others offend you, take the initiative to forgive them even if it is not requested. Some avoid forgiveness saying, "Well, he hasn't asked for my forgiveness." Don't wait for them to ask. Get rid of that baggage. The delay of forgiveness only hurts you.

If you forgive, act like it. Avoid replaying and reliving the issues. To me, to speak of past wounds is like ripping them open again. It doesn't help me. When and if I do share them, I do it only to help others learn vicariously, know they are not alone in their struggles, and that moment-by-moment forgiving and forgetting is possible.

TAKE ACTION: Request Forgiveness

When you know you have genuinely offended someone, make an appointment with the person you offended, be present in a calm way, and ask for their forgiveness. When you ask for forgiveness, follow this model: *[Person's name], I would like to ask for your forgiveness for [specific offense]. Will you forgive me? (Wait for answer.)*

In actual practice it might sound like: "Jeff, I am sorry for speaking so disrespectfully to you. Will you forgive me?"

It's that simple... and that hard. Say no more and no less about the offense. Don't try to explain the whys and wherefores. Don't defend anything you did even if there is a legitimate defense. I've made the mistake of trying to defend or offer excuse, and believe me, it only torpedoes your efforts.

Do not say, "*If* I offended you..." or "I am sorry *if* I offended you." You either did or you did not. If you didn't there is no need for the conversation. When there is a real need for an apology, there is no need for *if*.

Be sure the person considers themselves offended and is in need of an apology. Some things to which you might take offense may be non-offensive to others. Avoid checking for an offense unless you are already aware it exists; you will likely become aware soon enough. If the other person is behaving in a passive-aggressive, pouty way toward you, say something like "I've noticed you seem a little [tense/withdrawn/frustrated] lately. How can I help?"

Take responsibility for your part of the problem. From a systems perspective, we are never without responsibility of some kind for any situation. Even if you are only .001 percent responsible, you are responsible. Accept it, seek forgiveness where needed, and move on.

Be aware that when you ask "Will you forgive me?" the answer can be no, like the one I got from Pastor George. If that is the case, you have done all you can. You can say, "I thank you for hearing me out and I hope you can find the grace and compassion to forgive me at some point in the future."

Their refusal to forgive only hurts them, and is an attempt to punish you, again. So let it be. Delete any communications that remind you of the situation and go forward. Move on to your next thoughts, next actions, and next achievements.

Let me remind you that conversations about offenses and forgiveness are best done in person. Using email or texting for these communications is not advisable. A phone call is a very distant second to an in-person conversation, and only serves as a last resort. Make an appointment to see the person.

Forgiven, But Things Are Different

Forgiveness does not mean that everything returns to the state it was before the wrong. It does not mean you act as if nothing happened. Time has passed, experience is gained, and learning has occurred.

A woman I know was sexually abused repeatedly by several family members. She could continue to be embittered and angry, but instead has forgiven and lives a full and happy life. Nothing, however, returned to the state it had been before the wrong. Though she has forgiven her abusers, she has been changed forever—relationships will never be the same; trust will not be restored; the memories, ongoing pain, and damage from the wrong remains; and she will always be on guard at some level, regardless of the relative safety of a particular setting.

Forgiveness does not always mean that reconciliation can occur or that reconciliation is wise. If you had a relationship before, you may be reconciled at some level, but trust must be rebuilt. Reconciliation requires effort on the part of all parties. And reconciliation does not always mean forgiveness has occurred. It can simply mean that the issue has been swept under the rug.

Faith Sticky Note: **Forgiveness**

Forgiveness is an extremely important matter to God. He went to great lengths and sacrifice so that you and I can be forgiven by Him.

God commands me to forgive because it is good for me and good for others. I want to be forgiving because He wants it and I trust Him to know what's best. He wants me to forgive as He forgave.

> *Be kind to one another, tender-hearted, forgiving each other, just as God in Christ also has forgiven you.*
> —Ephesians 4:32 (NASB95)

As hard as it is to forgive, it just makes sense. Sometimes when I feel unable to forgive and am hounded by thoughts of unforgiveness, I take a deep breath and pray, saying to God, "I can't, but you can make it real in me." I have been greatly helped and changed by this simple prayer.

For an interesting parable that illustrates God's forgiveness, ours for one another, and God's response to our actions, read the parable in Matthew 18:23-35.

Chapter 14

Develop a Powerful Support Team

Two are better than one,
because they have a good return for their labor:
If either of them falls down,
one can help the other up.
But pity anyone who falls
and has no one to help them up.
—Ecclesiastes 4:9-11

"I do it myself" is the expression of a normally developing two- or three-year-old, but not always wise for developing adults. When, as a result of pride, unhealthy independence, or feared embarrassment, adults also say "I do it" and fail to access the support of others, they can end up lonely and ineffective.

As you work toward living without regret, you will benefit from gathering people around who can support, guide, and encourage you, and serve as sounding boards.

Who is on your support team?

Who do you still need on your team?

Mentors

When departing on his epic journey as described in Homer's *Odyssey*, Odysseus, King of Ithaca, called on a man named Mentor to groom his son, Telemachus, to be the next king of Ithaca.

So *mentor* has come to refer to someone who advises, guides, and trains by offering the benefit of their experience. The mentoring experience can be a formal or informal relationship, more or less structured, and may or may not involve an institution. In order to ensure advancement, individuals seek a mentor who is powerful in their organization to assist them.

Some believe that a mentor must be older than the protégé. I suggest that a mentor need only be qualified by more experience in the area of focus. In some instances a mentor can be chronologically younger than the protégé; I have several younger mentors.

How Do You Get a Mentor?

Find someone you trust, respect, and is or has been where you want to go in your life or in your work. Ask them to be your mentor. Work with them for a while. If the relationship is not working, discontinue and find another mentor.

Your direct supervisor is usually not your best mentor because there are power issues at play, and your supervisor holds influence over your evaluation, advancement, paycheck, and your job in general. This influence keeps you from being sufficiently open with them for the relationship to really help.

How Do You Become a Mentor?

You simply ask someone to allow you to serve as their mentor. I am sure a feeling of discomfort has arisen as you read this, since most view asking to be a mentor as overly self-promoting. It all depends on your attitude. If you plan to carry a know-it-all, "I'm going to fix you" attitude into the relationship, then fix *your* attitude or don't be a mentor. If you can see yourself as a servant to the protégé, simply make the offer and let the protégé decide. If you find the relationship is not working, discontinue it and find another protégé.

During the early and middle adult years there is a psychosocial developmental task that psychosocial theorist Erik Erikson describes as "generativity versus stagnation." I like to say that you can invest in future generations through giving back, contributing to help people develop in various aspects of their beings, and acting to make the world a better place. Or you can stagnate and produce nothing but a stinky pool of self. The goal is to land somewhere between the two and be an individual who demonstrates caring toward others and their future as well as caring for self. Mentoring and being mentored are a part of the "generative" experience, and can be lifelong experiences.

Coaches

Get a coach. No, not a football or basketball coach (unless that's what you need). A life or business coach can help you think through, make decisions, and move toward your life, career, or business goals more efficiently. A coach can also help accelerate the progress you are already making or are poised to make.

A coaching relationship gives the client time and a safe space for thinking. It's like pressing the pause button for time to think deeply, in a bigger way, and plan for action beyond the daily grind.

I strongly suggest that you engage a coach who is credentialed or working toward a coaching credential. This is evidence that the coach is strongly committed to giving their clients the finest of service. In addition, credentialed coaches are required to commit to a uniform code of ethics that governs professional practice.

Expect the coach to be of quality character, trustworthy, and clearly present in the moment with you to listen and ask great questions that evoke thought and new awareness. Expect them to speak to you in direct terms as needed; encourage you; support you; assist you in planning, designing actions, and goal-setting; help you manage your progress; and hold you accountable as needed and desired.

If your coach seems not to be a fit or you are making big efforts but not making progress, talk to your coach about it. **A good coach wants progress for you as much as you want it for yourself.** If they don't want this or are not effective for you, get another coach.

Therapists

You might be carrying some issues that run emotionally deep and are painful, or you might have a mental health issue that is disruptive to your functioning and progress. In such a case I recommend seeing a good therapist. Take courage, step out, and get help.

There was a day when seeing a therapist carried a stigma, but this is less so today. If you choose to see a therapist, I, for one, will be standing and applauding your action. The only reason for self-consciousness or embarrassment about therapy is if you don't get it when needed or you hinder someone else from getting it when they need it. Notice I wrote "when" not "if."

To find a therapist, ask for recommendations from your medical doctor or your pastor or call a reputable clinic or counseling center to see if they have what you need. Try to get more than one name from the person recommending, and ask why they made these particular recommendations.

Before scheduling an initial session with a therapist, inquire about their training, experience, credentials, professional affiliations, specialty of practice in terms of human development, issues treated, and how often they work with people who have issues like yours.

Choose a therapist with a license versus one who has a certification only, and choose a psychologist over a clinical social worker. You want a therapist who has been practicing for at least ten years. If you need medicine for your condition, see a psychiatrist rather than a general practitioner or a therapist with another specialty.

After the therapist's qualifications and competency are established, the most important issues are a good fit with you and your comfort level with them. Hold an initial session with the counselor and pay their fee, with the understanding that you are trying out the relationship. Ask if they have been in therapy themselves. (You want this answer to be yes.) You want a therapist with whom you can feel comfortable and at ease, and with whom you can be absolutely honest. Some will not suit your personality or be a good fit in general for you. If the fit seems poor, find another therapist and don't worry about hurting their feelings.

After finding a good fit, avoid bouncing from one to the other. Find one and stay with them. If you leave, leave them for good. Consistency in the long term is important.

Consultants

With the abundance of do-it-yourself information available on the internet, it's tempting to do most things for ourselves. But there is no substitute for the experienced professional attorney, accountant, financial planner, physician, or therapist.

I try to do a number of things myself. Around our house my plumbing is a legendary laughing matter. This, as with many things do-it-myself, takes me hours when it would take a plumber minutes. I've decided that my time is more valuable than the money it takes to get things fixed by a professional and not have to worry about them.

Professionals such as plumbers are really consultants. They are experts in their field who assess the situation, identify what's needed, make recommendations, and sometimes institute the solution to the need. Sometimes they are responsible for the outcome. My plumber is; my physician is not—I must act on his advice for a positive outcome to be credited to him.

If you need someone to tell you what to do or to do it for you, hire a consultant.

Friends and Family

Family, friends, and others can be part of your support team. These people will support you in different ways than a professional would. They can listen, encourage, support, offer input and perspective, and fulfill some of the functions of a mentor.

If they really love you, they will be very honest and not let you get away with much. They will help you hold your boundaries. They will hold you accountable for important things.

A key difference between family and friends and professionals is the agreement. When you enter into an agreement with a professional, they agree to deliver a product within professional boundaries. Friends and family do not make this commitment and do not have the same responsibility, and as a result they might not be as motivated about your needs and progress or observe healthy boundaries.

Harsh, Uninvited Criticism

If you have ever received uninvited criticism delivered in an abusive fashion, you may believe that inviting input for the future will be painful in the same way.

I would call you a real friend if you offered me some helpful information such as "You have something stuck in your teeth" or "Your fly is down" or "There's something hanging from your nose."

I regularly sat beside my boss in public gatherings, and we frequently spoke in whispers to fine-tune the proceedings. He was known to be verbally abusive toward me and others on numerous occasions, privately and publicly. One day he came into my office and out of the blue, in a stern, directive, and commanding manner, said, "Halitosis. You've got a problem with it. Fix it."

Ouch. After the burning embarrassment of realizing I had bad breath subsided, I thought about it. My dental health is excellent and I am very conscientious about oral hygiene. But I realized I had been enjoying sugary sodas before meetings and then blowing my breath in his face as we whispered. I wanted and appreciated the input and immediately took action to do something about the issue. But the input was not the problem. The manner in which it was offered was the problem.

Sometimes we lose sight of the message when the attitude and manner of the communicator is offensive, and we don't seek out any more messages since we believe they might be delivered with a similar harsh attitude and manner.

Invited, But Too Nice

Some people are too nice by nature, and others by choice, which translated means that they do not speak the truth when needed for fear the message will hurt your feelings or affect their relationship with you even if they speak it in a kind way. They might not be honest with you unless you set the context for honesty.

To access an honest, helpful perspective from others regarding yourself, you must invite it. A perspective offered about another's situation without permission is criticism.

I make a practice of inviting a few trusted individuals to serve as sharpening influences in my life, and I give them permission to speak frankly, honestly, and directly to me about what they see in my thinking, attitudes, and actions. These individuals must have demonstrated that they:
- Care about me
- Respect me as a person
- Respect but don't always agree with my opinions
- Share my values

- Are not manipulative, mean, or pushing their agenda
- Are in a growth posture themselves
- Are courageous enough to lovingly speak the truth to me
- Are safe and non-judgmental
- Hold what I say as confidential

I ask them if they will accept my invitation to investing in my life in this way. If they agree, I sit face to face with them, individually, to request and receive their feedback. These individuals can be professionals, friends, or family. Having such support has helped me beyond measure to keep my life in a posture of growth.

Blind Spots

As the driver of a vehicle, I try to be aware of all other vehicles around me. I look ahead, in the mirrors, and over both shoulders. But on many, many occasions I have heard the horn of someone who was in my blind spot. I missed them even though I was looking for them. We all have similar blinds spots in our thinking, attitudes, and behaviors.

It's important to invite help with this. I am not suggesting that you allow someone to become judge and jury in examining and ruthlessly criticizing your life. But we appreciate the caution of a horn blast from time to time to keep us healthy, effective, and out of danger.

Accountability

In my circles we talk a lot about accountability. It's a buzzword for checking up on people to be sure that they did what they promised or that they are living up to a standard they set.

Accountability is not forcing or dogging someone about what they should do. It is not discipline or punishment. Rather, accountability is lending support to an individual as they work toward *their* goals, such as the ones you have identified while reading this book. Accountability is not dragging or pushing someone. It's more like putting an arm around them and walking beside them toward their goals.

The few people I have invited to this task are not my judges or my disciplinarians, nor am I theirs. But by holding me to my commitments, they help me be my best self.

Getting Support—Reactive or Proactive

In research I conducted on mentoring, it appeared that most of the subjects sought mentoring reactively based on need rather than proactively based on a personal and professional growth plan.[16] My client Gary highlighted this in picturesque, earthy terms when he said:

> You know, I have to admit...I usually seek [help] after the fact...when the train wreck is over. Then I will find somebody and ask them how to fix the trestle. But I am hoping that I am getting better. Instead of being a reactive person I will be more proactive. ...I used to wait until after the fact...After they jerked the rug out from under my feet. But now, if I feel the rug moving, I go find out what is going on.

Do you engage help proactively or reactively? Which seems better to you?

Excuses and Roadblocks to Enlisting Support

I hear excuses and descriptions from leaders regarding roadblocks and self-sabotage that keep them from seeking the help of others. Recognize any of these?

- I am older than most and have all I think I need.
- Yes, I am interested but... the time... I'm not sure when I would find the time.
- I'm afraid people will think I am weak and inadequate or that something's wrong with me.
- People older than me are largely out of touch with issues I am facing personally and those facing contemporary congregations and businesses.
- Everything's going fine right now so I don't see any need for help.
- I can't afford it.
- I am tired and satisfied with the way things are going, so let's not "poke the skunk."
- I don't get this younger generation and don't know what they could offer an experienced person like me.
- I am afraid to ask someone to be on my support team.
- Why do I need a support team? Isn't this all just common sense? (A client of mine said it dawned on him that he was paying me to help him do things that were just common sense. He concluded, "The truth is that

without support we generally don't practice things that make common sense.")

Get the support you need if you want to make real and consistent progress toward your goals. Don't let anything hold you back.

Faith Sticky Note: Isolation

Dr. Philip Zimbardo, psychologist and professor of social psychology emeritus at Stanford, speaks to this:

> I know of no more potent killer than isolation. There is no more destructive influence on physical and mental health than the isolation of you from me and of us from them. It has been shown to be a central agent in the etiology of depression, paranoia, schizophrenia, rape, suicide, mass murder...
>
> The devil's strategy for our times is to trivialize human existence in a number of ways: by isolating us from one another while creating the delusion that the reasons are time pressures, work demands, or anxieties created by economic uncertainty; by fostering narcissism and the fierce competition to be No. 1.[17]

Support for one another is also encouraged by the writer of Hebrews:

> Let us hold tightly without wavering to the hope we affirm, for God can be trusted to keep his promise. Let us think of ways to motivate one another to acts of love and good works. And let us not neglect our meeting together, as some people do, but encourage one another, especially now that the day of his return is drawing near. —Hebrews 10:23-25 (NLT)

We really do need each other for support, encouragement, and strength, especially as we make it our goal to live without regret.

Chapter 15

Guard against Sabotage

*Those who say life is knocking them down and giving them a tough time
are usually the first to beat themselves up. Be on your own side.*

—Rasheed Ogunlaru

I frequently work with people who are in transition and identifying what they really want for their lives and careers. They are often reticent to go for what they want. They have a litany of reasons for *why they can't* versus *why they can*. A question that often breaks through the doubt is "What's holding you back?" As they think about the answer, they often find that their reasons for not going forward are their own self-sabotaging doubts and fears. Once they frame an action plan and are ready to establish first steps of action, I like to ask, "What could derail you?" This question has quite powerful, positive results. The client becomes aware of and alert to issues that have derailed them in the past and potential new issues for the future. Awareness of hazards is 90 percent of keeping the train of progress on the track. Then one should work on action plans to control the risk of getting off the track toward their goals.

This chapter is about becoming alert to an insidious issue that can slow or derail progress altogether: sabotage.

What Is Sabotage?

When you are working toward purpose, goals, and a healthy way of living, sabotage can come as a hidden, secretive, sly, or underhanded interference with your progress toward your goals. Sabotage can come from others. And it can come from the place you least expect.

A Source You Might Expect

Sabotage from others can be an intentional choice on their part. They might be jealous, overly competitive, or insecure, and don't want you to do well, so they plan to hinder your progress. This kind of sabotage can come like a gnat in the face that doesn't stop you but sure makes the going more difficult. It can also come like a boulder in the road that stops you cold.

Sabotage can also be a reactive, irrational response. As described earlier, those around you can become anxious about your purpose, boundaries, and progress. They might try to interfere in a variety of ways in order to control you and create a more comfortable situation for themselves by keeping the old you in place. Sabotage from others can look like gossip, speaking ill of you, obstructing resources, withholding needed information, or even plotting against you.

You might think you are the only one who gets sabotaged. Not true. You might think you never sabotage. Not likely true. We are human beings, naturally self-protective and often self-promoting. But we see these qualities as socially undesirable, so they go underground. Our self-protective and overly self-promoting actions become hidden and secretive. When they involve perceived competition with others, they can become sabotage.

My coworker, Phil, was twenty years older than I, and seventeen years my senior at our workplace. I had risen to a job that was on the same level with Phil and was being entrusted with more and more by our supervisor, while Phil was moved out of the loop on some things. At one point he confronted me, saying, "You have too much power."

From that time on, Phil began to sabotage my work on multiple levels. He whispered in my supervisor's ear that I was growing too powerful with the board and was scheming to get the supervisor's job. My supervisor's trust toward me eroded, exacerbating his already rage-filled behavior toward me. I left the job. Phil was the saboteur. He remained unscathed and worked until he retired from the organization.

A Source You Least Expect

Sabotage can also come from where you least expect it to: you. You can become the worst enemy of your personal development and progress to success. Everyone self-sabotages once in a while, some more than others. To avoid sabotage and its consequences (big-time regret), it is essential to be aware and alert.

Most people don't realize when they are self-sabotaging because the behavior has been in place for a long time and has become habit. Unfortunately the consequences of self-sabotage might not surface until even later, and by then the ditch is deep. Sometimes self-sabotage feels like the best thing to do, but you would not name the action "sabotage." You might say it was playing it comfortable or playing it safe.

Types of self-sabotage run the gamut from limiting beliefs and false assumptions to negative, discouraging self-talk; from self-medicating with drugs or alcohol to counterproductive self-soothing actions such as overeating. You can also self-sabotage with poor personal or social boundaries, self-absorption, emotional insecurity, false guilt (speaking to and about yourself with "shoulds" and "oughts"), being and acting to please others, workaholism, perfectionism, procrastination, and idealism (which leads to constantly unfulfilled expectations).

False Assumptions, Limiting Beliefs, Negative Talk
Your own thoughts and inner conversations can be among your greatest saboteurs. These conversations grow out of false assumptions, limiting beliefs, and ways we outright lie to ourselves. Self-sabotage can sound like:

I can't...

It has to be 100 percent (perfect) or nothing.

If it's hard, I must be going in the wrong direction.

If it will hurt someone's feelings, I shouldn't do it.

If I ignore the problem, it will go away.

Life must be fair.

If I fail, it's bad and means I am a weak person.

There are only a couple of choices in any decision.

I need to think and do what pleases others.

Growth and progress should be easy and painless.

I'll get it because I deserve it.

If people care about me, they should know my needs and meet them.
I have to...
I can't feel good until...
There is never enough...

Do any of these sound familiar? You may or may not say these things to others, but you likely say some of them to yourself. Inner conversations like these discourage you and drain your energy. You *learned* to talk to yourself this way and you can learn to talk a different way.

With practice you can successfully argue with your thoughts until you come to a better way of thinking. I recommend you have your support team close at hand, since you will likely be trying to starve out some deeply ingrained habits of thought.

I encourage people to discover the truth about their thinking. I ask questions that challenge their current thinking and help them explore other possibilities and create new awareness. When they seem stuck in a particular way of thinking, one of my favorite powerful questions is "How else could you think about this?" I don't tell them another way to think, because most people are able to discover for themselves ways to move from self-sabotage to more helpful perspectives and healthier thought patterns.

Overly Critical of Self

Another way we self-sabotage is by being overly critical of ourselves. Hypercritical self-talk in which we beat up on ourselves drains our energy, discourages us, and can lead to depression and physical illness. It shows up in our posture, our eyes, and how we behave in social settings. I find that it's good to name the emotion you are experiencing (more than once if needed), learn from experience, and move on to other things. This is no split-second project, by the way. It takes a little time. But you are building a habit for dealing with your own self-criticism.

I tend to be pretty hard on myself. But I am learning to pay attention to my inner conversations and speak to myself about myself with more grace and compassion. I extend this to others, and I decided I can do it for me, too. You are your most valuable responsibility. Pay attention to how you treat yourself and be kind. You'll enjoy being with yourself more, others will enjoy being with you more, and you'll be able to serve others more freely and effectively.

Anxious, Irrational Behaviors

Our anxious behaviors can also be self-sabotaging. There was a time when if you were angry with someone, you didn't have the option of picking up the phone; you had to write a letter. By the time you wrote the letter, you were often thinking and feeling better.

Today, however, you can tell someone off in a hurry by emailing or texting without having to look them in the face. You can be as angry as you want, but that's a form of self-sabotage—and a great risk for regret. Lashing out via text, email, or even phone doesn't create the productive communication needed for a relationship. It doesn't make you feel any better, and you might even become angrier as you replay the offense. If you press "send," you could damage a valuable relationship.

If you are worried about something, you can pace the floor or compulsively check email for news about the situation. This is self-sabotage. You are draining your emotional and physical energy toward unproductive ends.

In both of these cases, find something else to do that will distract you from your anger and worry. The specifics of this strategy are different for each individual. For me, watching a good movie helps. Talking to a friend can help, or finding something to do and think about in which I can be absorbed. Taking aggressive action toward my goals really helps. Once my anxiety has eased, I make better decisions and act in a better way to resolve the issue or be with it until it resolves.

Sacrificing Long-Term for Short-Term

You can also self-sabotage by sacrificing a long-term goal that you really want on the altar of a short-term goal that answers an immediate desire. This action can seem helpful at the time, but ultimately has the effect of interfering with your goals.

Cy was a very capable, competent, conscientious, and hard-working upper-level manager in a rapidly growing start-up business. From the beginning he was included in a management group that included the CEO.

As the business grew, other officers joined the firm and became a part of "the group." Cy felt threatened, especially when the newbies got to spend more time with the CEO than he did. With the business still grow-ing, everyone was busier. Job responsibilities become less general and more specialized in nature, increasing Cy's feeling of isolation.

Instead of actively putting himself out there and consistently cultivat-ing those relationships, Cy sabotaged his goal to be a vital, contributing part of the group by burying himself in his work, thus becoming more iso-lated and separated from the group. A period of coaching with me helped Cy recognize his actions as sabotage. He got out of his isolation and ac-tively contributed to the group at a level helpful to them and rewarding for him.

Putting Your Emotions in Charge

You can sabotage your progress by putting your emotions in charge of your thoughts and actions. If you have a negative emotion about a project, you can allow that emotion to sabotage your overall attitude, interest, motiva-tion, and progress toward the project. If you feel sad, you can allow this to slow you down. If you feel angry, you can act out in a way that sabotages your relationships and is destructive to your progress. If you feel afraid, you can be self-protective and unable to give your best energy to the project. You might want to fight, take flight, or freeze in the face of fear.

Emotions frequently do not correspond to reality, and they are more unpredictable than the weather. Don't allow your emotions to take con-trol of your being and acting. Choose to name what you are feeling and keep moving forward regardless of how you feel. Soon you will act your way into a different way of feeling.

If your emotions are particularly intense, dominate your thoughts, or clearly hinder your ability to function, I suggest that you find a good ther-apist who can assist you in working toward better functioning and prog-ress toward your goals.

Starving Self-Sabotage

Identifying a behavior as self-sabotage is a great foundational step to-ward removing it; starving out the behavior is a bigger matter.

Current brain research shows that neural pathways are constructed for new thinking and are strengthened through use. Pathways created but not used weaken and can be lost altogether.

Habits of self-sabotage by way of our thoughts and negative self-talk involve neural pathways that have been strengthened over time by frequent use. Cy's method of dealing with a sense of exclusion from the group had been his M.O. for years. It was his automatic defensive response. The neural pathways governing this behavior cannot simply be disconnected. Instead, other more desirable pathways must be built, and the former, less desirable pathways starved through lack of use.

A therapist once taught me a basic concept that revolutionized the way I deal with my thinking. It's called the 3 Rs: *Recognize, Remove, Replace.* **I pay attention to my thinking and have learned to *Recognize* unhelpful thoughts. I've realized that I cannot *Remove* them; they will just return if I don't consciously *Replace* them with other more positive and helpful thoughts.** Before acting on the 3 Rs, I may not feel very good because by the time I really notice what's happening, even when I am paying attention, I have already given myself a good, solid punch or two on the chin. But even though I may not feel like it, I act my way into a new way of feeling. In fact, I use the old "fake it till you make it" or "acting as if" strategies. I act the way I want to feel.

Be alert to and aware of sabotage. Often you can do little to control the sabotage of others but you can control *you*. Instead of interfering with your own progress and creating an opportunity for regret, get out of your own way by thinking, speaking, and acting in ways that support you in being more, seeing more, and achieving more.

Faith Sticky Note: **Even Jesus Knew Sabotage**

As I watch for sabotage, I am reminded that sabotage came frequently and from many sources in Jesus's life. Some of His saboteurs were those closest to Him—His disciples. They tried to prevent Him from fulfilling the mission given Him by the Father.

We can be our own saboteurs through dwelling on past mistakes, focusing on our weaknesses, doubting ourselves, and weighing ourselves down with discouraging and negative self-talk. The writer of Hebrews encourages that we "strip off every weight that slows us down, especially the sin that so easily trips us up" and run the race God has set before us, even when we are tired and it hurts, looking toward the finish line with Jesus as our example (Heb. 12:1-3). Paul, though he persecuted the cause of Christ at one point and had a good foundation for self-sabotage, refused to focus on the past and determined to press on in his mission for Christ (Phil. 3:13-14).

Be on guard for sabotage from yourself, your thinking, and others. Keep running the race toward completion of your mission.

Step 3

TRANSFORMING: Learning to Live without Regret

Even when you form your best plans and perform the actions required by your plans, you will experience feelings of regret because regrettable things do happen, and some are beyond your control. You can choose to avoid living with these thoughts and feelings of regret as constant companions and literally transform them into potential-filled learning opportunities for living a hopeful, meaningful, and purposeful life in which you realize your maximum growth potential.

Learning to live without regret is about being and doing. People who live this way persistently look for opportunities to learn and embrace them when they come. They also recognize that learning always involves change in their thoughts and actions that occurs in predictable ways.

Chapter 16

Heart for Learning to Live without Regret

Life is divided into three terms—that which was, which is, and which will be. Let us learn from the past to profit by the present, and from the present to live better in the future.

—William Wordsworth

A life without regret requires a growing awareness of and openness to the fact that regardless of age or stage of life, there is always more to be learned. Some of our greatest learning occurs as we encounter and work through challenging circumstances.

When we embrace this perspective, we are more likely to transform regret into a potential-filled, hopeful experience leading to a fuller, more meaningful, more purposeful life in which we realize maximum growth potential. This realization can make life an experience of active adventure in which no experience is wasted versus a perceived experience of passive victimization.

What kind of person consistently embraces such an approach to life?

Adult Learners in Their Development

People who can embrace this approach to life are primarily adults who are developmentally at least twenty-five years old. Whether or not they use the abilities, they are able to think systematically, logically, abstractly, and critically. They must also be able to think hypothetically, extrapolate, solve problems, and discover what a problem really is beyond its symptoms. These thinking skills can be improved with practice. A person need not be a superhero learner, just a bona fide adult learner.

Adult learning and *adult development* are practically synonymous terms. For the remainder of this chapter, I will use "learning" to speak of both. Adults approach learning in distinctive ways that impact their ability to live without regret. Do these basic assumptions about learning as set forth by Malcolm Knowles in *The Adult Learner* sound like what you do in your life?:

- **Adults choose what and when to learn.** They learn informally through experience, interaction with their environment, observation, and contact with more experienced individuals. Or they can choose the formal classroom for learning. Or they can use both. But most learning takes place outside of a classroom. Unless it is required reading for a class of some kind, the fact that you are reading this book is indicative of self-directed learning. Good for you!
- Adults have a **growing reservoir of experience** that serves as a resource for their learning and for assisting others in learning.
- **Interest in and motivation to learn** (readiness) is, for adults, strongly related to what they must do to continue maturing in their social roles (e.g. parent, employer, employee, friend, volunteer).
- As adults continue to mature, their learning becomes more **problem-centered** than subject-centered.
- Motivation for adults to learn **comes from inside them** and not so much from outside (intrinsic versus extrinsic motivation; desire versus performing for the sake of attaining a good grade).
- Adults want to know why it is important to learn a thing. They want to know **how it will help.** Knowledge for knowledge's sake is a lower priority.[18]

As an adult you can decide for yourself to learn about an issue and learn from the circumstances. You decide whether or not to adjust your perspective to transform regret into a potential-filled, hopeful experience. You have experience to help you. Your internal motivation to do a better job in your social roles, in solving your problems, and with your own sense of expediency in dealing with circumstances is your most effective motivator for learning.

The Attitude of a Learner

I make a distinction between the activity of learning and the quality of being a learner. On one end of the continuum are those who learn only because they have to do so to survive or relieve pressure or pain. On the other end are those who learn primarily because it is their way of being—a basic attitude of life. They are *learners-at-heart*. There are all measures of degrees along the continuum. A person can decide where along this continuum they prefer to live.

Learners-at-Heart

Learners-at-heart are motivated out of their very essence to be more, see more, and achieve more. Take a look at these qualities of the learner-at-heart and see if you find some of them in you:

- Interested
  - » Curious
  - » Wonder-filled
  - » Passionate about learning new things
  - » Attentive
- Open
  - » To new ways of thinking
  - » To adjustment in their beliefs (not necessarily religious), values, and attitudes

- Thinkers
  - » Critical
  - » Reflective
  - » Discerning
  - » Inclusive of other ideas
  - » Go beneath the surface to the deeper meaning and implications of experience
  - » Problem-finders (identifiers) as well as problem-solvers
- Steady
  - » Strong convictions, beliefs, and values developed out of their learning so far
  - » Emotionally able to change

- Proactive
  - » Turn life experiences into learning experiences
  - » Seek personal growth and development. Little is seen, heard, felt, tasted, touched, or experienced in any other way without something being learned from it. The primary question for the learner-at-heart is "What can I learn from this experience?" Once they milk it for all they can, their attitude is "Next!"

I am convinced that individuals who are deeply into this end of the continuum are rare. They give time and energy to clearly chart the course of their lives as they understand them in the moment. They monitor the accuracy of their course and progress toward their goal. They take time to reflect and pay attention to areas of needed growth in their lives. They are unafraid to admit their humanity, with all its inadequacies. They regularly reach outside themselves to engage a "sharpening influence" or an extra set of eyes to help them monitor their need for growth and progress toward it. They learn from their own mistakes and the mistakes of others. They believe that the best investment they can make is in their own development, and take a proactive approach to pursuing growth at every turn.

Learners-at-heart avoid regret, but not *all* regret, because they are proactive and interested regarding their personal development. They recognize that planning and acting on their plan is wise. When life's powerful, challenging, and difficult situations come to these individuals, they are ready. They have prepared ahead of the challenge. The way is not easy, but it is sure. When the threat passes, they remain vigilant in their watch for opportunities to become all they can be.

When regret comes to visit, they are not surprised and are already in learning mode. They readily and efficiently reframe regret into a hopeful, life-changing, potential-filled experience; and in cases of mistakes, they avoid similar mistakes in the future.

Some of the most vibrant, flexible, resilient, and energetic adults I have known are learners-at-heart all their lives. As they draw their last breath they are still learning and discovering things they never knew before. I want to be one of these.

Are you a learner-at-heart? Your answers to these questions can give you some indication:

- What have you learned about yourself today or even this week?
- About others?
- About your relationships?
- About your part in the world and history?

You can be a learner-at-heart. It is a choice and an attitude of life.

Learn When You Must

People on the opposite end of the continuum from the learners-at-heart tend to learn only when they must. At this end of the continuum are people who do not pay attention to what is happening in them and around them. As a result they can lack or lose focus, lack direction, get off course, and be unaware of opportunities for needful action toward personal course adjustment and growth. Some types on this end of the continuum are:

- The arrogant know-it-alls who believes there is nothing they need to learn
- Those fearful to admit they lack experience or knowledge so they put up the front of "no need." They are embarrassed to admit that they are indeed human and have significant growth points that need attention.
- Those pleased with the status quo and unwilling to put forth the effort to learn. They are too comfortable, lazy, and unwilling to make the effort to be all they can be. They view growth as uncomfortable, requiring work and shaking things up, creating a chain reaction of needed adjustment in other areas.
- Those who feel overwhelmed and helpless in the face of the immense complexity of our time and have a love for the status quo. They put their heads in the sand hoping all will work out in the end.

People such as these continue in their present state until they must face change, suffering, loss, life's inevitable challenges to their thinking and behavior, and even death. **They are often surprised by situations that prompt feelings of regret because they pay attention only sporadically along the way or fail to pay attention at all. They react.** Their attention becomes focused, adrenaline flows, senses heighten, and they take action for change in the midst of perceived threat, frantically reaching out for help. When the threat passes they return to busy-ness as usual and inattention, once again guarding their egos and laziness.

Those who learn only when they are forced to can experience regret. Their hope is that undesirable things won't happen, but they do happen. Their hope is that they won't have regret, but they encounter it more than they want to. They don't learn from past experience or vicariously from the experience of others.

When my wife and I lived in metropolitan areas, she described her strategy to avoid getting lost in the complex system of roadways this way: "I just find my little trail to each place and use it every time." Some people take this approach to development in life as a whole. They keep traveling the same thought and belief-system trails and avoid other needed trails which are the creative, the novel, and the out-of-the-box. Their famous last words may be "This is the way I've always done it."

Motivations to Learn When You Must

Though pressure and pain motivate anyone to learn, they are the primary motivations for those who learn only when they must. These motivations can be stated in other terms such as "to get more comfortable" or "to lighten the load" or "to improve my situation." The pain quotient must be pretty high to break through all of the personal and social issues related to admitting feelings of regret, admitting to issues related to the feelings, and being moved to work through the issues and get assistance in doing so, if needed. For some, pain and pressure are the only effective motivators for learning.

Honestly, I am not a fan of pain, but it is a ready and regular teacher of the lessons of life. It can test our belief systems as a whole and can call our attention to individual beliefs in our systems that are not working in experience. We choose whether or not to learn from pain.

Forms of pressure and pain are found in formal learning when one wants to get a good grade, a degree, a certification, or some other qualification. For example, I have some students who are in middle adulthood who are not tech savvy. My classes require them to learn to use a computer and basic software sufficiently to do their work, communicate with me, and communicate with one another for class. If it were not for the pressure, they would not likely go to the trouble to learn computer basics.

Those whose primary motivations are from pressure or pain are happy just to get out of the learning setting largely undisturbed. After formal education is done, large numbers of adults are reluctant to acknowledge any need for continued development beyond that which is absolutely necessary for maintaining the status quo. They are satisfied to know just enough to survive. They prefer the comfort of familiar ways and avoid change unless absolutely essential. They are happy to get by with the least disturbance possible, so they avoid novel thinking and challenges to their comfortable ways of being and doing. They fail to truly thrive, and their world narrows until they appreciate only a very tiny space in the midst of the wonder around them. Because things in the world around them are constantly changing, their status quo becomes a broken paradigm for living.

According to Helen Bee in *Journey of Adulthood*, maybe half of adults in Western culture think only some of the time at higher levels (involving abstraction, inference, problem-finding, and problem-solving).[19] We know that cognitive development continues into adulthood, so most adults are certainly capable of this higher level of thinking but don't practice it much because it is hard work. According to Knight and Sutton, they are more likely to perform at higher levels when supported and challenged to think at those levels.[20]

If you are at this end of the continuum, I hope you will learn enough to stay alive, but you will fall woefully behind the curve in your life and work in this fast-paced age of instant information and continual change. More than this, I hope you will gather the support you need to be more, see more, and achieve more in your learning and development.

I believe the "learning (changing) only when I must" attitude is a key reason that people don't see a counselor or health care professional as needed for strengthening health and wellness. It's why people stop reading and don't engage in continuing education (except as required by outside forces). It's why people have poor self-awareness, poor understanding of others, and poor self-care, and don't engage mentors and/or coaches. They want simple, easy, comfortable answers.

Inspiration

Inspiration can temporarily motivate some to learn. They get caught up in the emotion of a topic and are moved to learn more and take action. But the motivation for and application of the learning wanes with the decline of inspiration. I see this frequently in my coaching practice; a client gets fired up about an idea during a session and commits to learning how to accomplish it. At the next session, they may or may not have done something about it. Inspiration has evaporated in the whirlwind of daily life. As their coach, it is my job to hold their vision and hold them accountable for the commitments they have made to themselves, thus helping them transform their inspiration into action.

Contentment?

You might ask, "So when is it okay to be content with what you know and 'relax'?" "Can you still be a learner and be content?"

Remember, this is a continuum, and you can decide where along it is the best place for you. I lean toward the learner-at-heart side because I love learning new things. I believe it is better to be proactive and ahead of the game (though not compulsive) rather than behind the eight ball. I tend toward the novel, creative, and adventurous in learning more. It keeps my life interesting and rich. I'll let you decide how proactive you want to be and what works best for you in reaching your goals.

Whether your attitude is more like learning only when you must or being a learner-at-heart, you can be proactive in your learning rather than attending the school of hard knocks. Pick up a book. Attend a course. Join a study group. Get a coach. Seek out a mentor in your profession. Seek out a mentor for living to keep you in a proactive stance and out of that hard-knocks school.

But whatever you do, be more, see more, and do more to learn and develop to live a life without regret.

Chapter 17

How We Learn to Live without Regret

Real tragedy is having an experience
and missing the meaning.

—Robin Roberts

The most important ingredient in living without regret is the attitude you have about learning. Understanding the somewhat predictable processes of learning can help you better engage in learning to make difficult, "regrettable" experiences become hopeful and potential-filled.

We discover more about how learning takes place every day. The growing knowledge bases in the fields of educational psychology and neuroscience give us a framework for understanding how we learn. Here are some of those learning methods:

Proactively Add to Knowledge and Understanding

You can learn by simply adding knowledge and understanding to inform your beliefs, values, and attitudes through studying new material in a variety of contexts and through a variety of methods. This was our predominant way of learning in school.

Vicariously through Observation

You can also learn to avoid regret vicariously through observation. All human beings have the ability to learn vicariously. When you see someone who is like you succeed at an endeavor or avoid what could have been a costly mistake, you can try to follow the model of their experience. You attentively observe their actions, remember them, and replicate their behavior. You're following their example.

Using the same process, you can also learn to avoid mistakes or even injury and death through observation and learning vicariously. You don't have to make the same mistakes as those around you. Let someone else take the hard knocks. Learn from their mistakes.

Reflective Practice

Reflective practice is a way of learning practiced by adults and particularly in the professions. It involves reflecting *on* action after an occurrence has passed or reflecting *in* action while an occurrence is in progress. You take deliberate, conscious pause to reflect on what you have done and are doing, and make decisions about your effectiveness and what you will do differently in the future. This is especially powerful in experiences that result in regret. Reflective practice affects the way you approach the future, improve your skills, and increase effectiveness.

Transformative Learning

Even your most trusted ways of thinking and acting require adjustment and even transformation as you encounter new information, gain more experience, and change personally. *Transformative learning* is focused on transformation of a person's ideas, perceptions, and ways of thinking, and I believe such transformation is usually accompanied by emotional, cognitive, physical, social, and even religious expressions of grief. You will note hints at this in the process below.

Disorientation Creates a Dilemma or Crisis

Depending on the extent of one's life experience, much of adult learning centers on disturbance or "shaking up" of a person's current way of thinking and doing. Such disturbance is variously referred to as *disequilibrium* or *disorientation*.

The term *disorientation* is uniquely suited to adult learners because their extensive experience has allowed their way of thinking to become firmly established. On occasions when your established way of thinking doesn't work for making sense of life events or in the face of alternative opinions, you can feel disoriented. For adults, disorientation happens more often as a result of the interactions and challenges of day-to-day living than it does from the intellectual rigor of the classroom.

Because feelings of regret are so closely related to our thinking and expectations, situations of regret can readily create a disturbance in our way of thinking, as can positive experiences.

Take business owner Robert, who has a belief that all successful people are conscientious, orderly, on time, and efficient. Chuck, a new hire at Robert's company, is very creative and offers new and innovative ideas about serving their customers, which is exactly what Robert believed was needed. Chuck, however, is not conscientious, orderly, on time, or efficient. Robert started feeling regret about hiring Chuck, fearing that Chuck was not a successful person and therefore would not contribute to the success of the business. Then Robert realized that the qualities he needed for his business and the qualities he believed all successful people have were not neatly packaged in one person. Robert adjusted his thinking, making it more inclusive, and allowed for Chuck's style as successful. His business is more productive and serving customers better than ever.

Disorientation from Change

Any change, positive or negative, involves a measure of disorientation. The manner of doing and being that once worked for you cannot remain the same as before the change because the circumstances upon which you built your being and doing are now different. Therefore your thinking and acting must change. The old is lost (maybe with good riddance) and the new has come.

For example, let's say Joe's Burger Shack is your favorite place to eat and you go there with friends a couple of times weekly. You have a way of thinking about Joe's and its quality as related to other restaurants, and you have built a part of your weekly schedule around eating there. Then Joe closes his Burger Shack. Disoriented? Yes. You must choose a different favorite restaurant and change your schedule.

I commonly encounter churchgoers whose congregation has decided, for good reason, to change the way they have done a thing for the last twenty years. Such change is very disorienting and grievous for some. They can choose to change their thought and action and embrace the change, or continue to resist, create conflict, sow discord, and become known as a negative, complaining individual.

Confusion and grief of loss may explain our reluctance to embrace some changes. Those who are able to readily embrace needed change are more flexible, emotionally healthy, and resilient.

Disorientation from Life Events
Disorientation can come as the result of positive life events such as:
- Birth of a child
- Financial prosperity
- New job
- Becoming more healthy
- Acquiring a new social role (such as becoming a parent or business partner)
- Occurrences that don't make sense to us or that require knowledge and understanding we do not currently have

Disorientation from Exposure to Alternatives
Disorientation can result from exposure to:
- A new concept or idea
- A new way of doing things
- An alternative point of view
- Alternative values

Disorientation can also result from:
- A flash of insight
- The discovery that a personally held assumption or belief is false or limiting.

Here's a very simple example of disorientation from exposure to alternatives: You learn that a camel has only one hump. But then you see a camel with two humps. Something in your thinking must change to adjust to the new information.

Disorientation from Loss
Any type of loss brings tremendous, somewhat unexpected change, which has the effect of disorienting you and can generate feelings of regret. Loss can include the death of a family member or friend or the loss of health, a limb, financial stability, your marriage, a relationship, a job, possessions, or business. You can also experience disorientation when confronted with a sense of your own finiteness or mortality.

Disorientation can result from any of the above and any other situation in which your current way of thinking does not work to make sense of the issue or occurrence.

An example of disorientation from loss might involve the loss of your personal economy. You have learned to enjoy a certain standard of living and are quite comfortable in your job. You discover that you will be laid off. This is disorienting on a number of levels, and your current perspective will not continue to work. You must adjust to create a different standard of living for a time, create or refresh your résumé, search for a job, polish interview skills, retool for a new job, and keep things afloat while you do.

Moving toward Transformation

Disorientation creates a dilemma. The dilemma is that your current attitude and way of thinking is not working to make sense of your experience or has ceased to be sufficiently useful as a guide for life. It's like a crisis. Something must happen or adjust in order for you to move forward, stay healthy, and live without regret.

You can allow such disturbance of your thinking to devastate and confuse you, or you can use it as a springboard to learning to think and behave in a new way. Without such a shake-up, your motivation to learn can be very low and you might not learn readily.

You cannot remain in a state of disequilibrium or disorientation. *Reorientation* is necessary if you are to return to healthy functioning in life. Reorientation can be achieved as you critically examine your thinking and make the adjustments required for your thinking to serve as a better guide for your life.

When you're experiencing disorientation, a somewhat predictable process generally follows. You will likely engage in[21]:

- Self-examination, possibly with feelings of guilt and shame
- Critical assessment of your assumptions and perspectives; you feel alienated from related social expectations
- Recognition that others have gone through similar processes
- Exploration of options for forming new thoughts, roles, relationships, or actions
- Planning a course of action for new thoughts, roles, relationships, or actions
- Acquiring knowledge and skills for incorporating new thoughts, roles, relationships, or actions

- Trying out new thoughts, roles, relationships, or actions
- Building competence and self-confidence in new roles and relationships
- Reintegrating your thinking based on your transformed perspective

Using some or all of these aspects of critical reflection to address the crisis, various authorities on transformative learning note that an individual might:

- Stretch their current way of thinking to include new learning from the information or experience
- Add the learning as a new item in their thinking, thus adjusting the way they view the world
- Affirm their current way of thinking and acting in light of their heavy scrutiny as to its usefulness for guiding and making sense of life
- Reject the experience or information outright by ignoring it[22]

People move through this process at different rates. Your transformation can be immediate, or you can have breaks, interruptions, or setbacks in your progress. Eventually you must move through the process to achieve reorientation, equilibrium, and a state of healthy, realistic functioning.

In the transformative process, you might feel guilt or shame. You will likely be plagued with questions about personal competency whether or not you have been in the mainstream of socially acceptable thinking, and wonder how you missed the "truth" about the situation. "Confusion" might be a good way to describe this.

Your emotions must clear before progress out of the anxiety of regret can be experienced. They can be managed by rational thought. Moving out of disorientation requires rational, critical reflection on your thoughts and thought processes at every point. In the process you will realize that others have had similar experiences of disorientation and confusion.

As you feel more comfortable, you will start to explore what new thoughts, roles, relationships, and/or actions are needed. Talk with others. Engage in argument in an attempt to find a new way of understanding. Listen as openly as possible. Plan for action, get the knowledge and skills you need for your new way of living, and try out your new wings. You might make a decision or take some other type of action. As you do, build a sense of competence and confidence, and find the experience of reorientation.

Life-Stage Disorientation/Reorientation

When people reach about age forty-five, they realize they have about as much of life behind them as they have ahead of them. They have worked hard to make their place in their profession, but at this point they often realize that what they thought they wanted is not what they really wanted. This can be disturbing or disorienting for them.

Some realize they have not spent as much time with their spouse or children as they wish they had. Some realize that they are wealthy but have made no significant contribution to the world. Some come to coaching, where a coach supports them in working through their disorientation to a way of thinking and acting that is more desirable, productive, and healthy.

Those who have been working for some time to live without regret know that times of disorientation will come. They prepare for them by using the principles outlined in this book. They are not immune to disorientation, but they have developed plans to use it for good and to avoid regret. When regret does occur, they learn from it.

This Process Sounds Like Grief

I describe grief as "learning to live in a new way." Occasions for grief can initiate the transformative learning process. And the transformative learning process can be accompanied by the emotional stages of grief.

Elizabeth Kübler-Ross defined the emotional stages of grief that are typically demonstrated by those who learn they have a terminal illness or other experience of life-changing loss. Details of her model include:
1. Shock or disbelief
2. Denial
3. Anger
4. Bargaining—trying to find a way out
5. Depression—encountering the reality of the situation

6. Testing—searching for reasonable solutions
7. Acceptance—living in a new way in light of reality[23]

Some also add guilt among the earlier stages. Not everyone experiences all of the stages, and the stages do not occur sequentially or in a particular order. Rather you move into and out of the various stages toward the achievement of acceptance or living with the loss. The grief process is unique to each individual.

Be assured that all of these emotions are natural, normal, and require no apology to anyone. Feel what you feel, name it, embrace it, and continue to move forward as you work toward living without regret. The key concern in the emotional process of grief is getting stuck in one of the stages. If you find yourself stuck, see a therapist.

A young man in his early twenties was tragically killed in an automobile accident as he traveled from home back to the university he was attending. His grieving mother, Dorothy, repeatedly asked, "Why did God do this?" Her perspective was that God was a loving God who takes care of everyone and is in control of everything, including her son. Now her way of seeing God and the world was disoriented. How could God be loving and caring and *kill her son*?

Dorothy struggled to make sense of this horrible tragedy. Her current attitudes and thoughts were not working and needed to change. But instead of moving through the transformative process and exploring other thinking about how the situation might become hopeful and potentially good, she chose to remain in a highly emotional state (anxious). She chose to be stuck in the belief that God was responsible for the death of her son and therefore He was not the loving, caring being she once believed He was. She was stuck in deep regret.

Most people believe that tough times are only incidental, and they endure them in hopes of better days. Though tough times can be filled with regret and doubt, they are not just an unfortunate spill on the tapestry of life or a wrong-colored thread in its weave. Tough times are a natural part of life's fabric and have their place in creating its beauty.

In tough times you can whine, be depressed, be discouraged, or play the victim. Or you can make tough times meaningful by learning from them. Some things you can learn from tough times are:

- To pay attention. When times are good, we are likely to cruise on auto-pilot and pay less attention to the really important things. Tough times hit the pause button like a sledgehammer and we're jolted off autopilot and shaken into paying attention to what matters. Tough times have an interesting way of clearing the clutter.
- The reliability of what you are trusting. If you trust in something prov-en and unchanging, your confidence in this will be tested and can be strengthened. For me, this is my faith in God. I forget and doubt. Tough times remind me of His reliability.
- The value of clearly established foundations (definition of self, values, vocation, mission, and vision). In tough times these are tested over and over again. When they are clear, your foundations are your anchors. When they are unclear, you may feel adrift.
- The strength of your commitment to your foundations. If your commit-ment is strong, you can move forward with clear, focused direction. If your commitment is weak, it is only as good as writing on paper, and you can find yourself still searching.
- Who your friends are. When times are tough, your real friends come closer. There are only a few; others drift away.
- Who is with you. This might be your support team, and not necessarily your friends. During tough times, a professional or skilled individual can often help more than friends can.
- You are not the only one trying to make sense of it. When people wit-ness your tough times, they try to make sense of it by asking "Why?" They try to gain understanding, accurate or not, that helps them get more comfortable with the situation. A better question for you might be "What's next?"
- The strength of your own health and life skills. In tough times you are more resilient if you have excellent self-care along with powerful life skills for self-management, reflection, and productive action.
- Pain is a valuable teacher.
- Stillness and quiet in your inner self allows helpful insight to surface.

Just like you, I have experienced the disorientation of loss and change, and I have certainly learned from the school of hard knocks. In fact I have a diploma from there (seriously).

I have determined that I will embrace with hope the difficult circumstances in my life and view them as potential-filled learning experiences. This removes the feeling of regret. Though I have certainly not arrived at a regret-free life, it is a choice I have made.

Faith Sticky Note: Painful Experiences

Can you imagine how disorienting the acts of God must have been during the Exodus? Hearing Him speak out of a burning bush, witnessing the plagues of Egypt, feeling the spray of the water as He stood before the parted the sea in order for millions to cross it on dry land, experiencing the provision of daily food in the wilderness...

And what about Jesus's earthly ministry? Seeing Him heal the sick, eat with outcasts, touch lepers, appear alive from the dead...

Here are ten helpful (but hard) questions for when you are disoriented:

- What do I believe, know, and value that affects my response to this?
- How did I come to my thinking, beliefs, and behaviors regarding this?
- What are the facts related to the issue?
- What are my assumptions about this?
- How do I know my assumptions are valid?
- How have I integrated the Scripture, honestly and accurately interpreted, into my perspective about the issue?
- How do I know that my perception about this is true and accurate?
- Why would it be wise to question my perception about this?
- Why do I care about holding to this perspective?
- Should I revise or not revise my perspective?

Chapter 18

Now What?

I can't think about that right now. If I do, I'll go crazy.
I'll think of it tomorrow... I can stand it then.
Tomorrow, I'll think of some way...
After all, tomorrow is another day.

—Scarlett O'Hara in *Gone with the Wind*, by Margaret Mitchell

Just Another Book

Many read books like this one but rarely get around to acting on the principles and incorporating them into their lives. It's a lot to do alone, and the desire gets lost in the whirlwind of living.

Some are required to do this type of planning and take action as an assignment for a class. But, by their admission, they do just enough to get the grade and get out. Their work has little if any meaning to them.

When individuals engage their support team or a coach, they usually do hard work that is of higher quality, more meaningful, more helpful, and more enduring than they would have done on their own or for a class. **They discover ways to be more, see more, and achieve more.**

You Are at Choice

Now that you have read *Without Regret*, you are at choice. Will you do the hard work of implementing the practices to live without regret, or will you open the way wide for regret to occur and then live with it as an all-too-often companion?

You have fresh knowledge and understanding. What responsibility will you take for it? What will you do with it? Only you can be responsible for implementing, applying, and creating your own results. No one can do it for you.

You may feel overwhelmed at the thought of engaging in this journey. The challenges I've provided might seem so daunting that you feel if you deal with them now you'll go crazy. You may be tempted to put it off until tomorrow or the day after tomorrow.

None of the work recommended in this book is easy or creates overnight transformation. It's not magic. But the principles are effective. Real, meaningful change is hard work and takes time. Establishing and living on foundations such as these and facing difficulty as a learner takes diligence and courage.

Take Action Now

My request is that you take action now to form and perform your plans, and transform regret. It's a process, and this "journey of a thousand miles" starts with the first step. The very action of taking one small step is empowering, and the momentum from that one step can help you move to the next. As you act, you learn.

I hope that *Without Regret* provides you with some of the inspiration you need to springboard into implementing these practices. As we have noted earlier, inspiration is a short-lived motivator, so I also hope you will find the personal discipline and support to make these practices a part of your lifestyle.

Your initial work will not be pretty, clean, precise, or glorious. It might be very ragged and rough. But in the process you will smooth it and clean it up. Action is the priority—not a smooth and clean product. And the time to take action to live without regret is now, because the only guaranteed time you have is this moment.

Most people need some support and help in getting into action and making good progress, so here are a few tips that might help:

Some Attitudes to Keep in Place
- You are a whole, competent, capable individual.
- This is a marathon walk, not a run or sprint.
- Baby steps are steps. When you take enough baby steps, you go a long way.

- When it comes to life, there is no such thing as a finished product, only a product in process.
- Be at peace with initial work that might seem more like manure than magnificence.

Step by Step

STEP ONE: Put your support team in place.
1. Identify and engage the individuals/professionals you need for support and accountability. Give them permission to ask you about your work.
2. Create a contact/reporting plan that includes the frequency and times when you will let them know of your progress.

STEP TWO: Plan for planning.
1. Create deadlines for completing the planning work in Chapter 1 and developing a crystal-clear, written statement of your:
    a. Definition of Self
    b. Values
    c. Vocation
    d. Mission
    e. Vision
2. Establish regular times for planning. This might include a personal retreat or a little time daily to reflect and plan. Take one item at a time beginning with definition of self.
3. Execute this plan. If you already have a plan in place, go directly to the next step.

STEP THREE: Assess your current position. Rate the items below on a scale of 1-10 (1 = not at all; 10 = fully):
1. How aware and appreciative are you of your personal uniqueness?
2. How clearly defined are your relationships with others?
3. How clear are your boundaries?
4. How well do you practice assertiveness to protect your self-definition?

5. How well do you live by priorities that honor your definition of self, values, vocation, mission, and vision?
6. Are barriers or hindrances such as perfectionism or sabotage keeping you from moving toward your goals?
7. How well do you care for yourself?
8. How effectively do you deal with conflict situations?
9. How free are you from the clutter of unforgiveness? Do you forgive others? Do you forgive yourself? Do you seek forgiveness?
10. How much are you a learner-at-heart?

STEP FOUR: Identify items from Step Three on which you will focus. You can't change all of this at once, so try one of the following strategies:

1. Pick one of the above items and work on it. The item must be
   a. One for which your rating was less than you desire.
   b. One that, if you make progress with it, will result in a domino effect, affecting many of the other items. **OR**
2. Pick one or two items that you rated high on the scale and bring them up by a point or two. At the same time pick an item at the low end of the scale that is presenting a real problem for you, and work on that one. Do not focus on more than three of the items at once.

STEP FIVE: Actions to apply to focus items.

1. Establish times to simply reflect on the other items about which you need greater definition and clarity.
2. Clarify, commit to, and celebrate your:
   a. Personal uniqueness
   b. Relationships with others and how you will be without regret
   c. Boundaries
   d. Self-care
3. Practice
   a. Assertiveness
   b. Managing priorities
   c. Self-care

4. Breathe deeply and keep plodding, clarifying, committing, celebrating, enjoying life, and breathing deeply, plodding, clarifying, etc.
5. Report to your support team.
6. Repeat items 4 and 5 until you reach your goals.

Write It Down

When you work on these principles and have new ideas, please write them down. I heard a saying that makes complete sense in light of current brain research and my practical experience: "The shortest pencil is better than the longest memory."

Benefits of Forming, Performing, and Transforming to Live without Regret

When you work with these principles, you will very likely:
- Lay a foundation that can position you, your family, and future generations to make a big difference in the world
- Show up with people as more hopeful, grateful, and empowered
- Have a brighter countenance
- Live in a more evenly paced, uncluttered way
- Resign from a victim mentality
- Make decisions that are more often for the "best" versus the "good"
- Discover that some decisions are much simpler to make
- Lower your stress level in some areas
- Eliminate things you may be tolerating
- Remove from your life people and things that drain you
- Clean up your life physically, emotionally, socially, spiritually, and mentally
- Discover that you are able to build reserves of energy in your life physically, emotionally, socially, spiritually, and mentally
- Learn to love yourself and others more

Integrity, Despair, Wisdom

Should you live into late adulthood, you will naturally look into life's rear-view mirror. Erik Erikson, psychosocial theorist of the twentieth century, noted that depending on how we choose to view our lives, we experience something along a continuum between integrity and despair.

Integrity, in this context, refers to a person's ability, as they approach the end of life, to integrate their life experiences, make sense of them in light of the whole, achieve a positive evaluation of life, and be satisfied and content with it. No one does this perfectly.

On the other end of the continuum is despair, regret, feelings of failure, a focus on the shortcomings of life so far, fear of death, and the realization that there is not enough time to create alternatives to regret. The life question might be "So is that all there was to it? What was the point?"

You can choose to live with integrity rather than with despair. You can choose wisdom. You can see the good and the not-so-good in your life—the desirable and undesirable actions and incidents—and say, "I have lived well and I have learned much. I am wiser for having lived through my experiences. I am fulfilled."

Position yourself now to avoid despair and be able to look back on your life with a sense of integrity and wisdom, and without regret. Decide what you really want. Establish your mission and clarify your values. Increase your self-awareness and social awareness. Improve your self-management and social management. Keep learning and growing. Be more, see more, and do more to live a life without regret.

Faith Sticky Note: **Unrecoverable Regret**

I believe that there is one regret from which a person cannot recover. That one regret is turning one's back to God and rejecting His unmerited grace as extended to us in His unique, one-of-a-kind Son, Jesus Christ.

He lovingly and graciously offers this opportunity for right relationship with Him as a gift to us. Like any other gift, it is not earned or deserved. We received it by faith.

Time and space are not eternal. There will be a point when time and space roll back into eternity and will be no more as we know it. Our life itself is finite. One day we will die and no longer have the opportunity for decision or action. Then the window of opportunity to accept God's offer will close.

You can plan, act, and learn to avoid this unrecoverable regret by receiving God's loving offer of a relationship with Him.

Please contact me for more information on this important part of living without regret. I hope you will consider this carefully, take action on it, and live without regret now and for eternity.

About Dr. Michael Godfrey

J. Michael Godfrey DMin, PhD, PCC is the founder and president of True Course based in Robinson, Texas. Founded in 2003, True Course specializes in mentoring, coaching, and consulting services for businesses and churches. Dr. Godfrey is the designer of True Course Mentoring, a nationally recognized, award-winning mentoring approach that has received the "Malcolm S. Knowles Award for Outstanding Adult Education Program" from the American Association of Adult and Continuing Education.

In addition to True Course, Dr. Godfrey also serves as a part-time lecturer at the George W. Truett Theological Seminary at Baylor University. He is a senior certified, experienced consultant for the Birkman Method®, and the author of more than 47 published articles and chapters related to his revolutionary work.

Dr. Godfrey holds the Professional Certified Coach credential from the International Coach Federation with more than 1,000 clock hours of coaching individuals to achieve what they really want in life.

Dr. Godfrey holds a Doctorate of Educational Psychology with specialties in adult education, mentoring, creativity, and problem solving from the Baylor University School of Education as well as a Doctor of Ministry degree from Southwestern Baptist Theological Seminary.

A native of East Texas, Dr. Godfrey has more than 35 years of experience in Christian ministry. Dr. Godfrey and his wife, Susan, reside in Robinson, Texas, and have two grown children.

For complete information about Dr. Michael Godfrey and True Course Ministries, Inc., please visit www.DiscoverYourTrueCourse.com.

Endnotes

1   Perry, W. G. (1970). *Forms of Intellectual and Moral Development in the College Years: A Scheme*. Austin, TX: Holt, Rhinehart and Winston; Perry, W. G. (1981). "Cognitive and Ethical Growth: The Making of Meaning" in A. W. C. Associates' (Ed.) *The Modern American College*. pp. 76-116. San Francisco: Jossey-Bass.

2   Richardson, R. (2008). *Becoming Your Best: A Self-Help Guide for Thinking People*. Minneapolis, MN: Augsburg. pp. 2-4.

3   http://faculty.washington.edu/chudler/facts.html

4   Carter, R., Aldridge, S., Page, M., & Parker, S. (2009) *The Human Brain Book*. New York: Dorling Kindersley Limited. p. 39.

5   Zenger, J. (2008). *Developing Strengths or Weaknesses: Overcoming the Lure of the Wrong Choice*. Orem, UT: Zenger-Folkman.

6   Cain, S. (2012). *Quiet: The Power of Introverts in a World that Can't Stop Talking*. New York: Crown. p. 21.

7   Levinson, D. J., Darrow, C. N., Klein, E. B., Levinson, M. H., & McKee, B. (1979). *The Seasons of a Man's Life*. New York: Knopf; Levinson, D. J., & Levinson, J. D. (1996). *The Seasons of a Woman's Life*. New York: Ballantine.

8   Richardson, *Becoming Your Best*, p. 2, 4.

9   Wolpe, J. (1958). *Psychotherapy by Reciprocal Inhibition*. California: Stanford University Press, pp. 53-62, 72-75.

10   Zander, R.S., & Zander, B. (2000). *The Art of Possibility: Transforming Professional and Personal Life*. New York: Penguin. p. 31.

11   Loehr, J., & Schwartz, T. (2001, January). "The Making of a Corporate Athlete." *Harvard Business Review*. p. 123.

12   Ibid., p. 125.

13   Ibid., p. 123.

14   Brown, B. (2010). *The Gifts of Imperfection: Let Go of Who You Think You're Supposed to Be and Embrace Who You Are*. Center City, MN: Hazelden.

15   Gerzon, M. (2006). *Leading through Conflict: How Successful Leaders Transform Differences into Opportunities*. Boston: Harvard Business School Press.

16   Godfrey, J. M. (2005). "The Role of Mentoring in the Developmental Experiences of Baptist Pastors in Texas: A Case Study." Unpublished Doctor of Philosophy Dissertation, Baylor, Waco, TX.

17   Zimbardo, P. (1980). "The Age of Indifference." *Psychology Today*. August 30, 1980. pp. 71-76.

18   Knowles, M. S., Holton, E. F., III, & Swanson, R. A. (1998). *The Adult Learner* (5th ed.). Woburn, MA: Butterworth-Heineman.

19   Bee, H. L. (1996). *Journey of Adulthood* (3rd ed.) Englewood Cliffs, N. J.: Prentiss Hall. p. 168 as cited in Merriam, S. B., & R. S. Caffarella (1999). *Learning in Adulthood: A Comprehensive Guide*. San Francisco: Jossey-Bass.

20   Knight, C. C., & Sutton, R. E. (2004). "Neo-Piagetian Theory and Research: Enhancing Pedagogical Practice for Educators of Adults." *London Review of Education*, 2(1), pp. 47-60 as cited in Merriam, S. B., R. S. Caffarella, et al. (2007). *Learning in Adulthood: A Comprehensive Guide*. San Francisco: John Wiley & Sons.

21   Mezirow, J. (1991). *Transformative Dimensions of Adult Learning*. San Francisco: Jossey-Bass, pp. 168-169; Merriam, S. B., Caffarella, R. S., & Baumgartner, L. M. (2007). *Learning in Adulthood: A Comprehensive Guide* (3rd ed.). San Francisco: John Wiley & Sons; Cranton, P. (2006). *Understanding and Promoting Transformative Learning: A Guide for Educators of Adults* (2nd ed.). San Francisco: Jossey-Bass, p. 20

22   Mezirow, J. (2000). *Learning to Think Like an Adult: Core Concepts of Transformation Theory*. In J. Mezirow & Associates, *Learning as Transformation: Critical Perspectives on a Theory in Progress*. San Francisco: Jossey Bass, p. 3-33

23   Kübler-Ross, E. (1969). *On Death and Dying*. New York: Routledge.